# DECORATIVE
~ *painting* ~

*of the* World

# DECORATIVE
## ~ painting ~

## of the World

EBURY PRESS
LONDON

First published 1993
1 3 5 7 9 10 8 6 4 2
© World Living Arts Pty Limited

First published in the United Kingdom in 1993 by
Ebury Press, Random House, 20 Vauxhall Bridge Road,
London SW1V 2SA

Random House Australia (Pty) Limited
20 Alfred Street, Milson's Point, Sydney
New South Wales 2061, Australia

Random House New Zealand Limited
18 Poland Road, Glenfield
Auckland 10, New Zealand

Random House South Africa (Pty) Limited
PO Box 337, Bergvlei, South Africa

Random House UK Limited Reg. No. 954009

A CIP catalogue record for this book is available from the
British Library.

**Publisher**: Tracy Marsh
**Artist**: Glynne McGregor
**Art Director**: Stan Lamond
**Project Coordinator**: Gillian Souter
**Design Consultant**: Vicki James
**Photographer**: André Martin
**Production Director**: Mick Bagnato

ISBN 0 09 178236 8

Printed in Hong Kong by Mandarin Offset

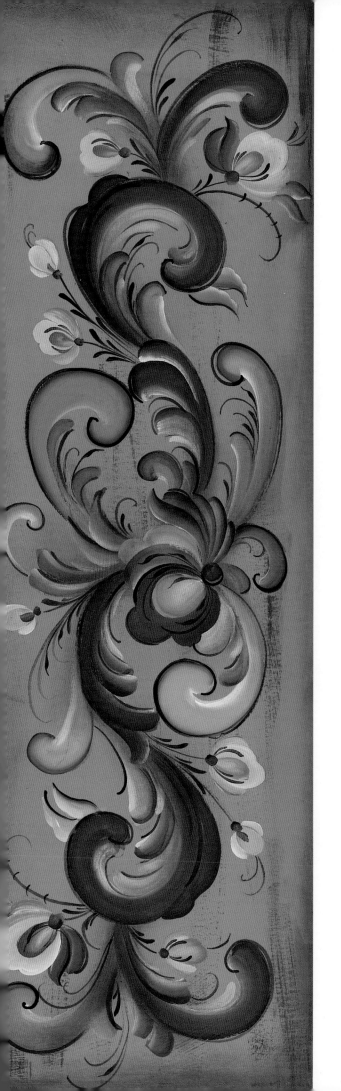

# CONTENTS

# ABOUT THIS BOOK

*As long as people have had homes, they have decorated them with paint or pigments. Drawing images from everyday life and using the colours of a traditional palette, ordinary people have striven to brighten their surroundings and express their sense of belonging to a cultural group. The embellishment of domestic objects and surfaces in this way is sometimes called folk art or, more commonly, decorative painting.*

Remarkable similarities can be found in the history of decorative painting. The ancient Egyptians used many techniques common to eighteenth century Bavaria, such as woodgraining and false marbling. However, the development of painting in each society very much depended on the

*Mexican plate*

materials available and contact with outside cultures. Even within Europe, great stylistic differences arose between such neighbouring countries as Norway and Sweden, or Germany and Poland. There is a clear pattern of influence along trade routes—the East on Dutch Hindeloopen—and along the paths of domination: the conquering Moors diverted Spanish decoration and, in turn, the conquistadors affected the art of Mexico. The study of cultural history through folk painting is a fascinating one.

In many societies there is no distinction between decorative painting and fine art painting. Even in the West, this discrimination is relatively new and possibly shortlived, as decorative painting is enjoying recovered status today. There is also a growing interest in the lifestyle of other countries; more and

more we are looking to cultures around the world for inspiration in decoration and design.

This book brings those two strands together by encouraging interest in decorative painting and inspiring the reader to draw from folk styles from around the world. To achieve this, the information it provides has been made as accessible as possible.

Each chapter looks at a different painting tradition, either of a region or of a cultural group. The opening pages provide insight into the heritage of those people and the Designs and Variations spread offers a wealth of ideas for adapting designs, creating borders and varying the colour schemes. The projects then guide you through the painting stages to produce a piece in the style of that tradition. Each project is graded in the following way:

*Beginner*
*No painting experience required but you will need to refer to the General Information chapter*

*Intermediate*
*Requires some practice on brushstrokes before undertaking the project*

*Advanced*
*Includes difficult brushstrokes and will require some skill*

The General Information chapter explains how to scale designs, prepare surfaces, paint different brush-strokes and finish your masterpiece. A colour chart is included, giving a recipe for each project colour using a small range of basic colours. There are twenty-five pages of designs, ready for tracing and transferring, plus a comprehensive glossary and index to help you find your way around the book.

*Lascaux cave paintings in the Dordogne region of France are an early example of decoration with coloured pigments.*

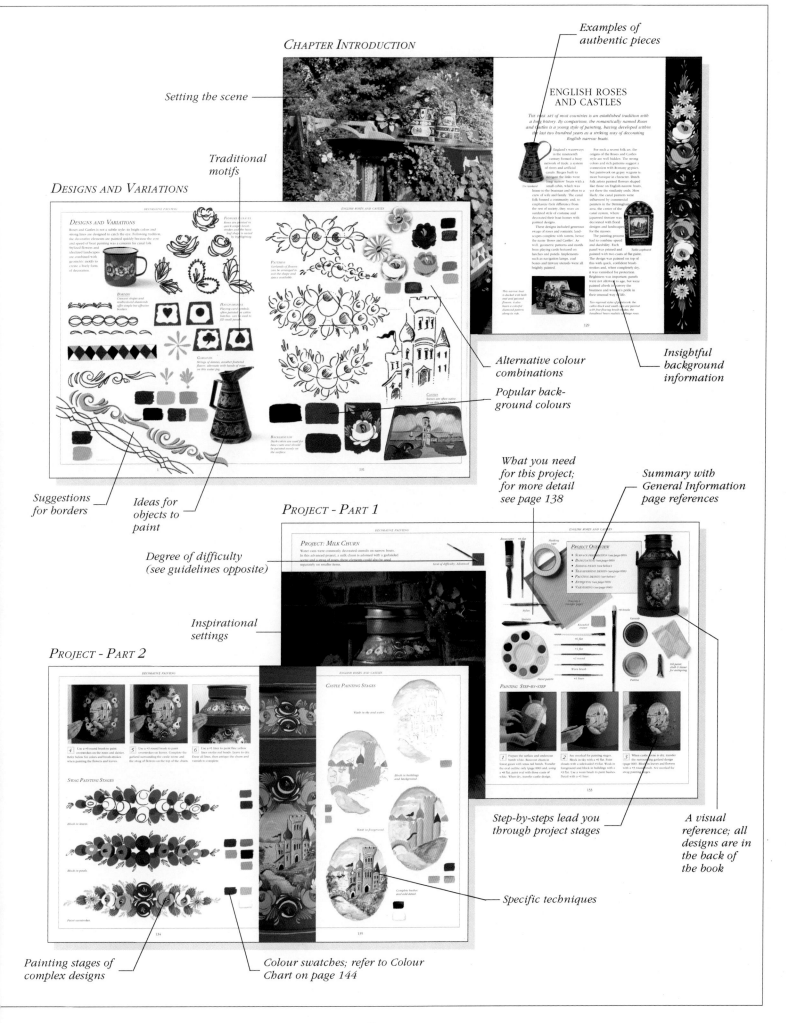

CHAPTER INTRODUCTION

Setting the scene ——

Examples of
authentic pieces

ENGLISH ROSES
AND CASTLES

Traditional
motifs

DESIGNS AND VARIATIONS

Alternative colour
combinations

Insightful
background
information

Popular back-
ground colours

Suggestions
for borders

Ideas for
objects to
paint

PROJECT - PART 1

What you need
for this project;
for more detail
see page 138

Summary with
General Information
page references

Degree of difficulty
(see guidelines opposite)

Inspirational
settings

PROJECT - PART 2

Step-by-steps lead you
through project stages

A visual
reference; all
designs are in
the back of
the book

Specific techniques

Painting stages of
complex designs

Colour swatches; refer to Colour
Chart on page 144

# AFRICAN TRIBAL ART

*THROUGHOUT THE WORLD, traditions of folk art are handed down through succeeding generations. In Africa, each tribe's traditions of belief, art and ceremony distinguish it from neighbouring tribes. This has resulted in an exciting array of styles, designs, symbols and displays of colour in African decorative painting. Here, art is not a separate arena of life, but an essential form of individual and tribal expression.*

The earliest forms of African painting can be seen even today on rock faces and in the caves of the Sahara desert. These works of art depict the people, tools and activities of daily life, and animals: the elephant, rhinoceros, antelope, ostrich and giraffe. Today, artists still decorate small stones, creating a design which emerges from the rock's natural shape: a curled cat or other animal.

*Beaded neckbands*

Many everyday implements, including combs, bobbins, spoons and bowls, are decorated to reflect social status or simply for their aesthetic appeal. Ceremonies play an important part in tribal life and the face and body are often painted with ochres for festivals or rites of passage. Ceremonial objects such as drums, weapons and masks are lavishly painted and adorned with beads, feathers and bones.

When western-style settlements developed, the exterior walls of homes, particularly those facing communal courtyards, were often decorated with pigments. Colours had different powers: red ochre enabled communication with one's ancestors; white, particularly around windows, protected against vengeful spirits. Today, earth pigments have generally been abandoned for acrylic paints and whole South African townships are alive with dramatic wall paintings.

The decorative art of Africa strikes us as fresh and un-complicated; apart from the early influence of ancient Egypt, it is a highly original style. It is no wonder that western artists such as Picasso, who sought to break away from the Renaissance tradition, found in it a rich source of ideas and images. Perhaps the greatest difference between the two traditions is the way in which art is perceived: in Africa, the process of creation is valued more highly than the finished piece.

*Branded gourd*

*The colours of a Ndebele wall mural match the traditional costumes of the women for brilliance.*

*Ceremonial shields in earth colours*

9

# DESIGNS AND VARIATIONS

African artists delight in combining contrasting colours, which are frequently separated from one another by black or dark brown outlines. Animals are sometimes depicted, but geometric shapes are the basic unit in African design. For some tribes, these bear a symbolic meaning; for others, they are simply pleasing to the eye.

### HATCHING
*Striking banded designs can be taken from these pokerwork bowls.*

*burnt umber*   *cinnamon*   *yellow oxide*

*yellow*   *ultra blue*   *xmas red*

### SYMBOLS
*For the Nsibidi tribe, repeated triangles and diamonds signify the leopard and his spots.*

### COLOURWAYS
*The combination below features in the project overleaf.*

*apricot*   *cream*   *dusty blue*

### BORDERS
*Triangles can be connected in a variety of ways and repeated with great effect, as on this shield.*

10

### FOLK CRAFTS
Inspiration can be drawn from other crafts such as beading or the cut-pile raffia work of the Shoowa tribe.

### GEOMETRICS
Simple elements—dots, circles, triangles and diamonds—create a rhythmic feeling and a sense of symmetry.

burnt umber · raw sienna · cream

### CONCENTRICS
Small geometric shapes, either hollow or filled, are embellished with lines around them.

### VIVID COLOURS
Natural pigments such as ochres and plant dyes provide a surprising range of intense colours.

# PROJECT: AFRICAN POT

The simple lines and natural colours of this design make it an
attractive starting point for new painters. This piece is made
of basecoated papier-mâché; a sealed terracotta pot would
also be suitable.

*Level of difficulty: Beginner*

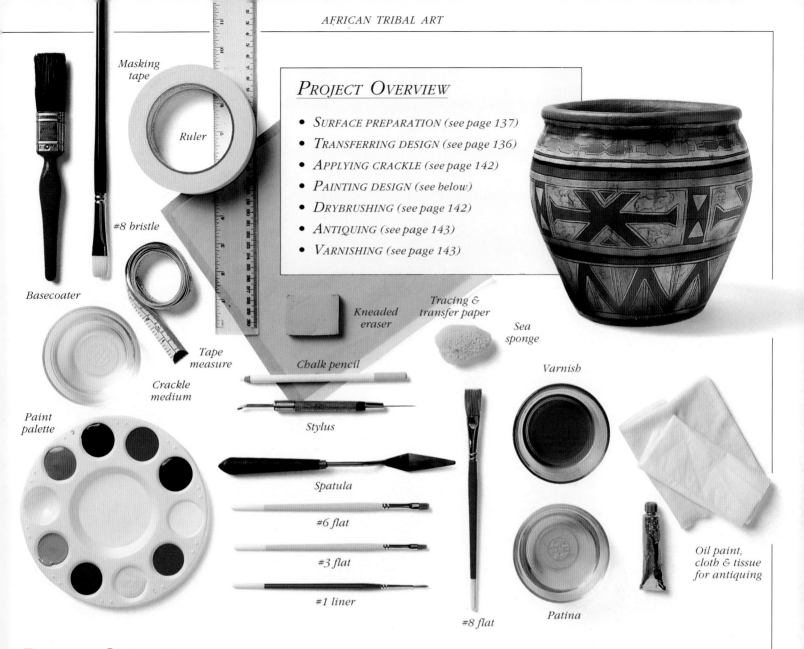

Masking tape

Ruler

#8 bristle

Basecoater

Crackle medium

Paint palette

Tape measure

Chalk pencil

Stylus

Kneaded eraser

Tracing & transfer paper

Sea sponge

Varnish

Oil paint, cloth & tissue for antiquing

## PROJECT OVERVIEW

- SURFACE PREPARATION (see page 137)
- TRANSFERRING DESIGN (see page 136)
- APPLYING CRACKLE (see page 142)
- PAINTING DESIGN (see below)
- DRYBRUSHING (see page 142)
- ANTIQUING (see page 143)
- VARNISHING (see page 143)

Spatula

#6 flat

#3 flat

#1 liner

#8 flat

Patina

# PAINTING STEP-BY-STEP

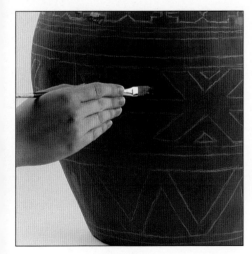

**1** Prepare the surface as appropriate. Transfer the design (page 146) freehand with a tape measure and ruler. With a #8 bristle brush, apply crackle medium to major colour areas.

**2** Block in cream, apricot and dusty blue where shown. Use a sea sponge to cover crackled area and a #6 or #3 flat brush in other areas as appropriate. Leave to dry before continuing.

**3** Use a #1 liner to paint narrow bands and detail in dark brown. Leave to dry. Use a #8 flat to drybrush burnt umber at random. When dry, erase lines and antique. Varnish to complete.

# MEXICAN PAINTING

*MEXICO is a land of bright colours and dramatic history. Vibrant sunsets, luscious fruits, vivid flowers, and birds with resplendent plumage have inspired Mexico's decorative painters to juxtapose brilliant hues. The vast heritage of Mexico's ancient cultures and its conquistadores also provide a wealth of motifs and designs. The folk art of this country is as striking as its origins.*

*Lacquerwork*

Art played an important role in the pre-Hispanic civilizations of Mexico. The pyramids and temples of the Aztec and Maya carried brightly painted sculptural reliefs and large frescoes of mythical animals. A wealth of information about their world is provided by pictorial manuscripts, or codices. These documents, painted on to deerskin or bark paper and then folded concertina-fashion, were decorated with highly stylized images of gods, rulers and warriors. The arrival of the Spanish in 1519 marked the destruction of the Aztec empire but, in remote areas, many Indian communities retained the customs of their ancestors and, today, crafts are an essential part of life.

This mix of the functional with the decorative is seen in the labour-intensive art of lacquerworking. Fruit from the calabash tree has a hard rind which provides villagers with bowls for food and drink. Once dried, the inside of the gourd is smeared with oil from chia seeds and coated with a coloured paste. The surface is then decorated with brilliant flower, bird and animal motifs and sealed with oil. In the village of Olinala, dishes, trays, screens, boxes and trunks of pine and sweet-smelling *linaloe* wood are lavishly decorated. Here they also practise the art of *rayado*: painting two coats of lacquer in contrasting colours, scratching a design with a thorn or needle, and then scraping away the topcoat to reveal the image.

*Papier-mâché doll*

Some forms of painting have changed over time. Nahua villagers who once decorated pottery now paint striking landscapes on handmade bark paper, combining fantasy with realism. Papier-mâché dolls and animals abound, all in bizarre shapes and garish colours. Popular painting is found in fairs and markets or on shopfronts and houses and reflects the Mexican love of beauty and ornament.

*Against a backdrop of bark paintings, a Nahua child paints pottery for market.*

*Mayan fresco, depicting daily activities*

# DESIGNS AND VARIATIONS

The palette of the Mexican painter is a vivid one: purples and pinks are combined with bright greens and startling yellows. The images are also startling: colourful skeletons and devils abound during the Festival of the Dead, while everyday art is a profusion of birds, animals and brilliant flowers. Decorative painters can also draw inspiration from the ancient art of the Aztec and Maya civilizations.

## GEOMETRICS
*The ancient step pattern below is the basis of the project overleaf.*

forest green

sunflower

xmas red

white

## CONTRASTS
*Mexican style allows and even encourages garish combinations.*

sunflower

aqua

cinnamon

## CURIOUS ANIMALS
*Carved wooden figures painted with bright spots add a lively touch.*

## BIRDS
*The double-headed eagle of Otomi embroidery is just one of the bird designs available.*

16

**PRACTICAL DECORATION**
In Mexico, the functional and the decorative are one; everyday furniture is brightly painted.

**FLOWERS**
These bright floral motifs are inspired by the lacquerwork from Olinala.

forest green    rose pink    purple    white

**SUN-KING**
The image of the sun has become a classic motif in design.

**BORDERS**
Leaf and sun shapes can be adapted for repeat designs.

# PROJECT: MEXICAN CHAIR

Contrasting colours and matt textures are characteristic of
Mexico; in this design, three strong colours are combined in an
Aztec step pattern. This is a quick and straightforward project,
ideal for beginners.

*Level of difficulty: Beginner*

*Basecoater*

*Masking tape*

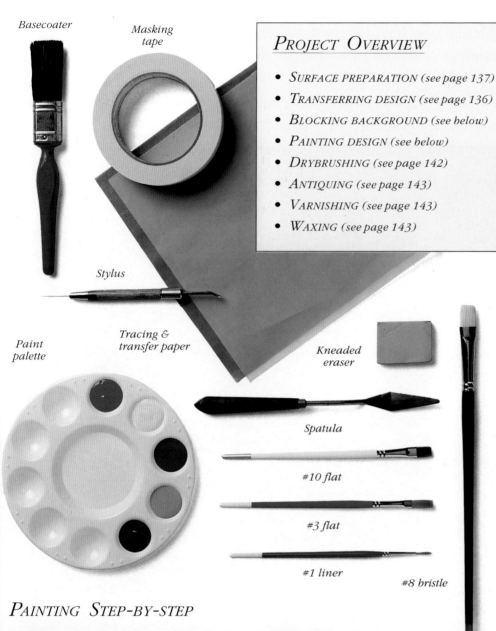

## PROJECT OVERVIEW

- SURFACE PREPARATION (see page 137)
- TRANSFERRING DESIGN (see page 136)
- BLOCKING BACKGROUND (see below)
- PAINTING DESIGN (see below)
- DRYBRUSHING (see page 142)
- ANTIQUING (see page 143)
- VARNISHING (see page 143)
- WAXING (see page 143)

*Stylus*

*Paint palette*

*Tracing & transfer paper*

*Kneaded eraser*

*Spatula*

*#10 flat*

*#3 flat*

*#1 liner*

*#8 bristle*

*Varnish*

*Wax*

*Patina*

*Oil paint, cloth & tissue for antiquing*

## PAINTING STEP-BY-STEP

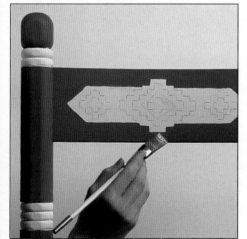

*1* Prepare the surface; if the chair is dark base colour, undercoat white with a basecoat brush. Transfer the design (page 146). Paint the background with two coats of cinnamon using a #10 flat brush.

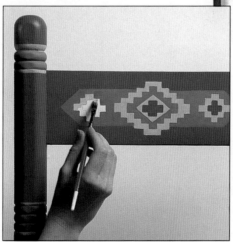

*2* When background is dry, block in the aqua, sunflower and cinnamon on the design using a #3 flat brush. Paint bands on chair rung with a #1 liner. Apply a second coat to the design and the bands.

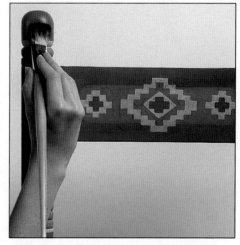

*3* Use a #8 bristle brush to drybrush burnt umber, emphasizing around the design and rungs and lightly over the design. When dry, erase lines and antique. Varnish the chair and wax to complete.

# PROJECT: MEXICAN WASHSTAND

Sky and earth colours are used to paint this bedside
washstand or cabinet. As well as the colour gradation, it
features the popular sun motif which could decorate a box
or platter on its own.

*Level of difficulty: Intermediate*

*Basecoater*

*Masking tape*

*Stylus*

*Spatula*

*Paint palette*

*Tracing & transfer paper*

*Sea sponge*

*Kneaded eraser*

*Varnish*

*Wax*

*#3 flat*

*#3 round*

*#1 liner*

*#8 bristle*

*Patina*

*Oil paint, cloth & tissue for antiquing*

## PROJECT OVERVIEW

- SURFACE PREPARATION (see page 137)
- BASECOATING (see page 141)
- TRANSFERRING DESIGN (see page 136)
- SPONGING GRADATION (see overleaf)
- PAINTING DESIGN (see below)
- DRYBRUSHING (see page 142)
- ANTIQUING (see page 143)
- VARNISHING (see page 143)
- WAXING (see page 143)

# PAINTING STEP-BY-STEP

**1** Prepare the surface. Use a basecoat brush to apply three coats of white. Transfer the design (page 147). Mask the door and apply the colour gradation with a brush and sea sponge; see overleaf for painting stages.

**2** Use a #3 flat brush to wash the borders in mauve and apricot and to paint an apricot band between the two sections of the design.

**3** Use a #3 round. Block pine and salmon petals and double-load leaves in turquoise and spruce. Block in cinnamon vase and, before dry, scratch with a stylus. Wash in ultra blue scrolls and pine sun (see overleaf for painting stages).

**4** Paint white circular patches scattered around the panel with the tip of your finger. Use a #3 flat brush side-loaded with burnt umber to shade the sun and stars.

**5** Paint cinnamon overstrokes on petals and cream on leaves with a #3 round brush. Paint teardrop strokes on the white patches and on apricot borders, in either turquoise or cinnamon, using the #3 round.

**6** Add detail in burnt umber with a #1 liner. When dry, use a #8 bristle brush to drybrush cream lightly around panels. Mix cinnamon and salmon and paint top of washstand. Erase lines, then antique, varnish and wax.

## SUN PAINTING STAGES

*Wash in with pine.*

*pine wash*

*Float shading colour.*

*Add cheeks and linework.*

*burnt sienna wash*

*peach*   *burnt umber*

## COLOUR GRADATION PAINTING STAGES

By using a sponge to apply paint, you can control the amount of colour and combine colours in a mottled effect. It is most effective on larger areas, particularly if a colour gradation is being applied. Sponge colours wet-on-wet.

*Sponge spruce at top and burnt sienna at base.*

*Overlap with mauve and salmon, moving towards centre.*

*Overlap with turquoise and apricot. Sponge white in centre.*

## SCRATCHING

Block in shape and, while the paint is still wet, scratch a design with a stylus or the end of a brush.

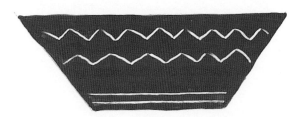

# ISLAMIC STYLE

*THE ISLAMIC AGE dates from the seventh century AD when the words of the prophet Mohammed were recorded as the Koran. Its influence spread across an enormous area, stretching from North Africa and Spain to Egypt, Turkey and Iran, and beyond the China Sea as far as Indonesia. An integral part of the religion is its expression in Muslim art, characterized by sophisticated colours and intricate patterns.*

*Sandalwood trunk*

From the twelfth century, strong colours adorned clothing, items of daily use, houses and entire mosques. The Koran forbade the carving of images or idols and this rule was extended to painting. As artists were not permitted to paint figures which cast shadows, they did not use shading to imply dimension, but used pure colours which have a brilliant, enamel-like sheen.

This same religious ruling encouraged the painting of patterns and abstract designs: even natural motifs such as leaves are stylized. Basic elements of Islamic design include polygons (geometric figures with many sides, such as a star or octagon), the arabesque (leafy foliage which twines in and out of a continuous stem) and calligraphy, or ornamental script. The first two can be repeated endlessly. The latter, once prized for its role in recording the word of Mohammed, now has a decorative value and is often impossible to read.

Muslim houses contain few pieces of furniture; seating areas are often built into the architecture and tiled, while cushions and rugs are used to create lounging areas. However, chests are commonly used to store clothes and belongings, and most homes have low tables on which tea and coffee are served. Morocco, which had an early French influence, developed its own tradition of more elaborate furniture carved from sandalwood and cedar. These pieces are painted with traditional motifs: a craft known as *zwaq*. Moroccan painters also draw on a unique palette, with darker and richer colours, including red, green and navy blue.

*A profusion of colour and pattern is created with paint, ceramic and fabric. Islamic doors are seldom left undecorated.*

*Jewellery cabinet*

Islamic design has many forms of expression: Turkish carpets, Egyptian textiles, Iranian ceramics and the mosaics which adorn so many Muslim buildings. All offer great inspiration for the decorative painter.

# DESIGNS AND VARIATIONS

Muslim painters are exceptional colourists and names such as turquoise, ruby and pistachio hint at the richness of their palette. To achieve extra intensity, semi-precious stones are often ground to powder for adding to paint. Although Islamic artists have a well-defined tradition of design, there are ample variations from which to choose.

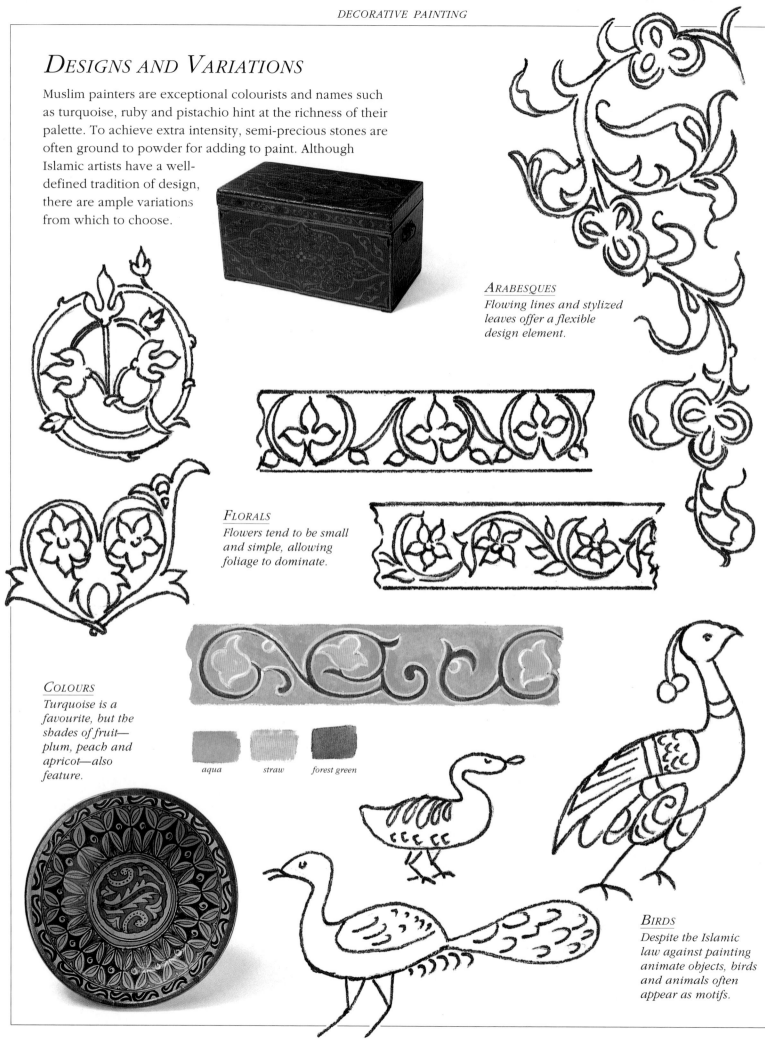

### ARABESQUES
*Flowing lines and stylized leaves offer a flexible design element.*

### FLORALS
*Flowers tend to be small and simple, allowing foliage to dominate.*

### COLOURS
*Turquoise is a favourite, but the shades of fruit— plum, peach and apricot—also feature.*

*aqua*     *straw*     *forest green*

### BIRDS
*Despite the Islamic law against painting animate objects, birds and animals often appear as motifs.*

## POLYGONS
Multi-faceted figures can stand alone or be incorporated in an endless pattern.

## CALLIGRAPHY
Script incorporated in designs is often ornamental rather than functional.

## ZWAQ
These painted shutters or mushrabiyya are an example of Moroccan work.

## BORDERS
Geometrics make ideal borders; the colours below feature in the project overleaf.

red oxide   olive   cream   red   spruce   French blue

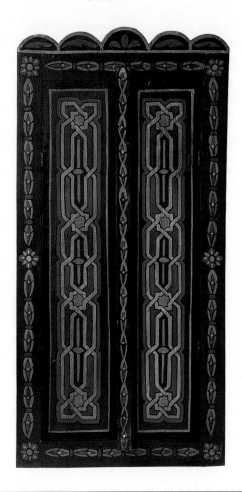

# PROJECT: MOROCCAN SHOEBOX

This typical Islamic shoebox is decorated with curling arabesques and flowers in rich Moroccan colours which are identified on the previous page. Despite the impressive appearance, this project is completed with simple brushstrokes.

*Level of difficulty: Beginner*

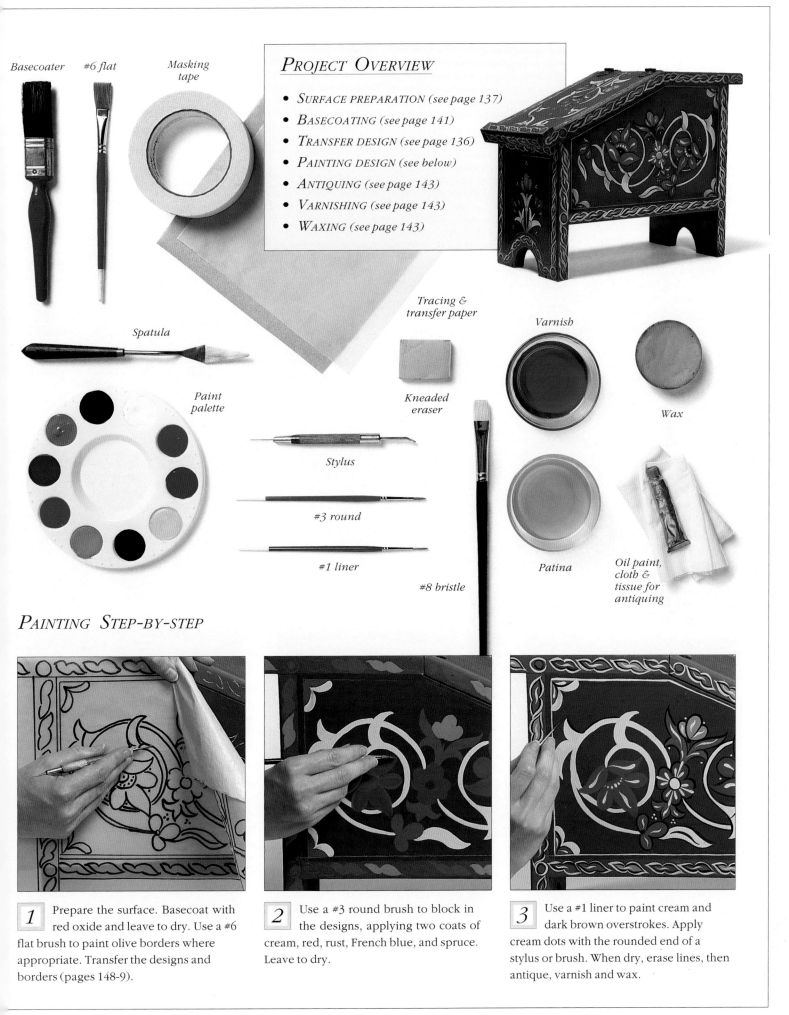

Basecoater  #6 flat  Masking tape

## PROJECT OVERVIEW

- SURFACE PREPARATION (see page 137)
- BASECOATING (see page 141)
- TRANSFER DESIGN (see page 136)
- PAINTING DESIGN (see below)
- ANTIQUING (see page 143)
- VARNISHING (see page 143)
- WAXING (see page 143)

Spatula

Tracing & transfer paper

Varnish

Wax

Paint palette

Kneaded eraser

Stylus

#3 round

#1 liner

#8 bristle

Patina

Oil paint, cloth & tissue for antiquing

## PAINTING STEP-BY-STEP

*1* Prepare the surface. Basecoat with red oxide and leave to dry. Use a #6 flat brush to paint olive borders where appropriate. Transfer the designs and borders (pages 148-9).

*2* Use a #3 round brush to block in the designs, applying two coats of cream, red, rust, French blue, and spruce. Leave to dry.

*3* Use a #1 liner to paint cream and dark brown overstrokes. Apply cream dots with the rounded end of a stylus or brush. When dry, erase lines, then antique, varnish and wax.

# PROJECT: TURKISH CASKET

An unusual painting technique has been used to transform
this papier-mâché box into a metal casket like those found in
Turkey. This 'metallic' relief work would also look striking on
a mirror frame.

*Level of difficulty: Beginner*

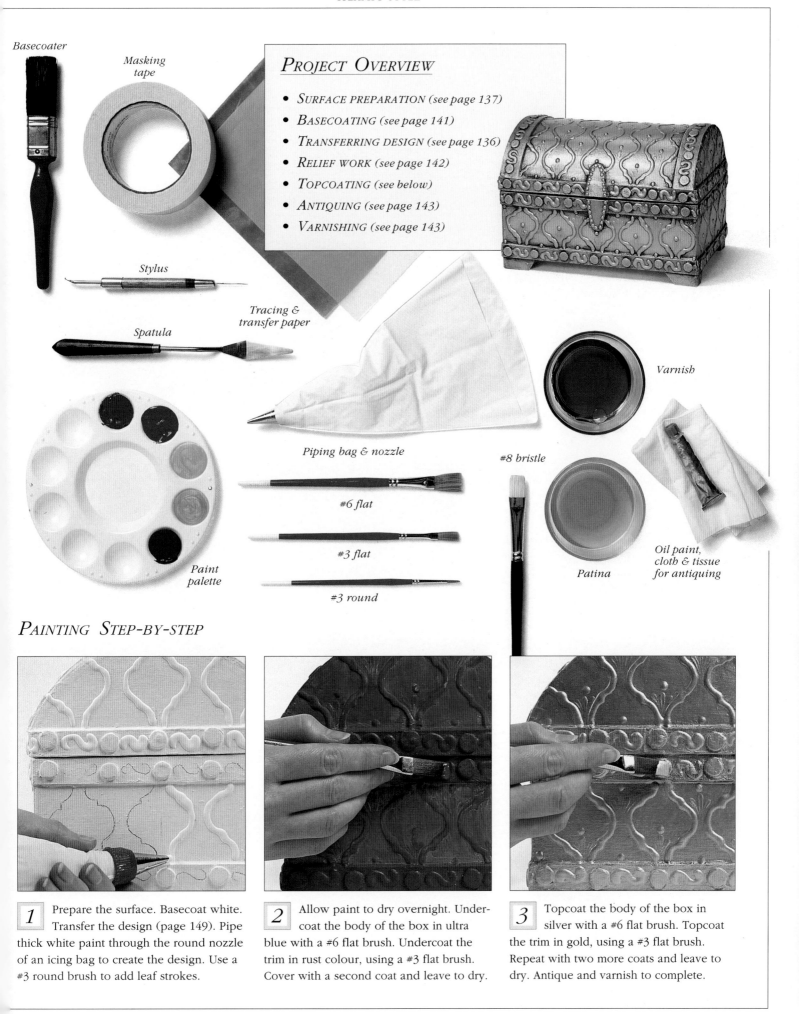

*Basecoater*

*Masking tape*

## PROJECT OVERVIEW

- SURFACE PREPARATION (see page 137)
- BASECOATING (see page 141)
- TRANSFERRING DESIGN (see page 136)
- RELIEF WORK (see page 142)
- TOPCOATING (see below)
- ANTIQUING (see page 143)
- VARNISHING (see page 143)

*Stylus*

*Tracing & transfer paper*

*Spatula*

*Varnish*

*Piping bag & nozzle*

*#8 bristle*

*Paint palette*

*#6 flat*

*#3 flat*

*#3 round*

*Patina*

*Oil paint, cloth & tissue for antiquing*

## PAINTING STEP-BY-STEP

*1* Prepare the surface. Basecoat white. Transfer the design (page 149). Pipe thick white paint through the round nozzle of an icing bag to create the design. Use a #3 round brush to add leaf strokes.

*2* Allow paint to dry overnight. Under-coat the body of the box in ultra blue with a #6 flat brush. Undercoat the trim in rust colour, using a #3 flat brush. Cover with a second coat and leave to dry.

*3* Topcoat the body of the box in silver with a #6 flat brush. Topcoat the trim in gold, using a #3 flat brush. Repeat with two more coats and leave to dry. Antique and varnish to complete.

# BAUERNMALEREI

*FOR MANY PEOPLE, the name Bauernmalerei is synonymous with folk painting. Certainly, the painting tradition which developed in the Bavarian and Austrian alps and the Swiss Apenzell was a strong one, spanning several centuries and influencing decoration widely. Bauernmalerei translates as 'farmer painting' but the farmer was more often customer than artist; most pieces were painted by travelling artisans or cabinet makers.*

*Spanschachtel*

Originally, simple designs were painted direct onto raw wood, either freehand or by stencil. Painted backgrounds were introduced to enhance cheaper woods and were sometimes used to conceal flaws and woodworm holes, although this was illegal in some areas. Favoured background colours were green and black, but the practice of painting an imitation wood grain using a paste—*kleister* in German—was also popular.

No part of the house was left undecorated. Bouquets or garlands were painted between windows on outside walls, while repeat designs often framed doors. Inside the home, armoires, chests for storing corn or clothes, bedheads and footboards all provided a painting surface. Personal belongings were often kept in *spanschachteln*, boxes made of thin shavings of wood bent around a mould. These boxes, given as gifts or as part of a dowry, might be painted with a portrait of the bridal couple or flowers.

Floral designs were a favourite subject, painted in exuberant bunches with blossoms too large for their stems. The simple Tölzer rose became a pattern for painters and tulips, imported from the East, were painted as a three-petalled flower to symbolize the Trinity. Religious scenes, pictures of the seasons or of secular life were sometimes featured on panels, though this required more skill on the part of the painter.

*Milking stool*

Trends in art and architecture trickled down to affect rural art. Renaissance designs were quite flat and heavily outlined. With the advent of Baroque tastes, much ornament was added, with leafy borders and brighter colouring. In the Rococo period, symmetry was discarded and scrollwork filled designs. Pale blue became popular in rustic art, though Bauernmalerei continued to be characterized by contrasts, combining greens and blues with yellows and reds.

*Painted and real alpine flowers complement each other on an Austrian home (left) and on a wall in Gryon, Switzerland.*

# DESIGNS AND VARIATIONS

The appeal of Bauernmalerei is in its rustic approach to decoration. Colour schemes can be sombre or garish, but rarely sophisticated. The subject matter is traditional but personalized by the addition of simple portraits and text. Lettering, an important element in design, might be used to date the painting, name the artist or the owner, or add a sentiment or scripture.

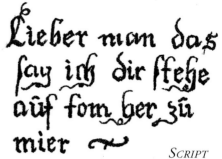

### SCRIPT
*Proverbs and expressions of love can add ornament to a design.*

### SPANSCHACHTELN
*A bridal couple adorn a dowry box as they have done for centuries.*

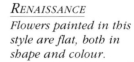

### RENAISSANCE
*Flowers painted in this style are flat, both in shape and colour.*

*yellow oxide*

*olive*        *tomato*

### HORSEMEN
St Florian rides by on this Austrian wall cupboard.

*pimento*

*black*

*forest green*

### BORDERS
Simple strip designs are worked in austere colours.

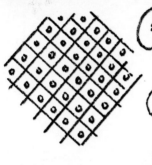

### DETAIL
Hatching and scrollwork can be added as ornamentation.

*black*  *rust*

*forest green*

### BACKGROUNDS
Green was popular throughout the Tyrol; Austrians favoured black as a background.

### THE HUNT
Hunting scenes were frequently painted, as on this elaborate wooden target.

35

# PROJECT: BERRY PICKER

After the rose, the tulip is the favourite symbol of
Bauernmalerei: here it is painted in a flat and primitive style
with little regard for realism. The repetitive design is ideal for
narrow panels or as a border.

*Level of difficulty: Beginner*

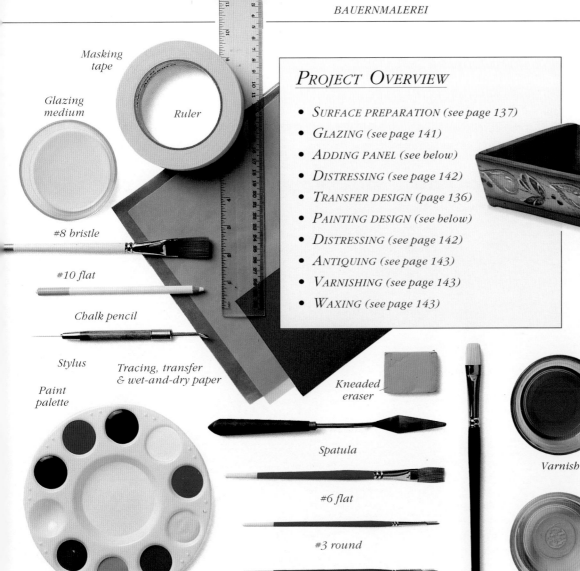

*Masking
tape*

*Glazing
medium*

*Ruler*

### PROJECT OVERVIEW

- SURFACE PREPARATION (*see page 137*)
- GLAZING (*see page 141*)
- ADDING PANEL (*see below*)
- DISTRESSING (*see page 142*)
- TRANSFER DESIGN (*page 136*)
- PAINTING DESIGN (*see below*)
- DISTRESSING (*see page 142*)
- ANTIQUING (*see page 143*)
- VARNISHING (*see page 143*)
- WAXING (*see page 143*)

*#8 bristle*

*#10 flat*

*Chalk pencil*

*Stylus*

*Paint
palette*

*Tracing, transfer
& wet-and-dry paper*

*Kneaded
eraser*

*Spatula*

*#6 flat*

*#3 round*

*#1 liner*

*#8 bristle*

*Varnish*

*Wax*

*Patina*

*Oil paint, cloth &
tissue for antiquing*

## PAINTING STEP-BY-STEP

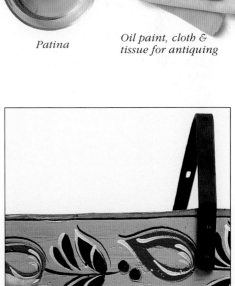

*1* Prepare the surface. Tint glazing brown earth and glaze the piece with a #10 flat, or coat with a brown wash. Leave to dry. Use a chalk pencil and ruler to mark appropriate panels on each side.

*2* Paint panels dusty blue with a #6 flat. When dry, distress panels with wet-and-dry paper. Transfer design (page 150). Block in fire red and Prussian blue flowers and teal leaves, with a #3 round.

*3* Paint white overstrokes with a #3 round. Add Prussian blue dots with fingertip and paint detail and trim with a #1 liner. When dry, erase lines and distress design lightly. Antique, varnish and wax.

# PROJECT: GERMAN CHEST

This Baroque project features several faux painting techniques to create an instant antique: woodgraining to imply an expensive timber, spattering and threadwork to suggest the activity of insects over time, and the application of an antiquing patina to further age the chest.

*Level of difficulty: Intermediate*

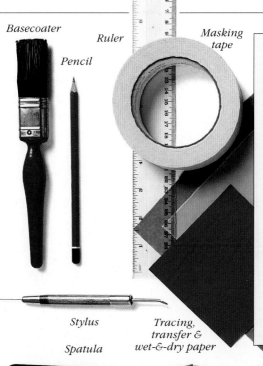

*Basecoater*

*Pencil*

*Ruler*

*Masking tape*

*Stylus*

*Spatula*

*Tracing, transfer & wet-&-dry paper*

*Paint palette*

*Kneaded eraser*

*Comb*

*Sea sponge*

*Thread*

*Varnish*

*Wax*

*#6 flat*

*#3 flat*

*#3 round*

*#1 liner*

*Toothbrush*

*#8 bristle*

*Patina*

*Oil paint, cloth & tissue*

## PAINTING STEP-BY-STEP

**1** Prepare surface. Mark panels with a ruler and pencil. Basecoat side and top panels in pine and front panels with three coats of white. Basecoat rust around the panels. When dry, topcoat forest green around panels and pine on moulding.

**2** Mask off all panels with tape and distress the forest green areas with wet-and-dry paper. Remove the masking tape. Transfer the design (page 150) onto one or more panels.

**3** Paint the design wet-on-wet, using a #3 round brush and a #1 liner as appropriate. Refer to the bouquet painting stages overleaf for colours and brush-strokes.

*4*     Tint paste with burnt umber and paint the top and side panels of the chest and the moulding with a woodgrain. Refer to the woodgraining painting stages opposite for details.

*5*     Use a #3 flat brush to paint panel border in rust. Paint trim line in pine with a #1 liner. Paint lettering in pine with a #3 round brush. Leave to dry, then erase all design lines.

*6*     Dilute burnt umber with water. Load a toothbrush with paint and spatter panels lightly. Dip thread in paint solution and create drag marks on the panels. Antique, varnish and wax to complete.

## Bouquet Painting Stages

*Paint foliage wet-on-wet. Allow to dry, then paint vase and flowers wet-on-wet.*

forest green

rust

pine

yellow

French blue

red

burnt umber

white

# WOODGRAINING PAINTING STAGES

There are as many techniques for imitating grains and knots as there are different types of wood. The basic principle is the same, that of laying down a thick tinted paste and making impressions in it. It is the selection of the tool that determines the pattern or grain. Crumpled newspaper or plastic wrap, combs, jagged brushes and cardboard shapes are all suitable tools.

*Seal with untinted paste.*

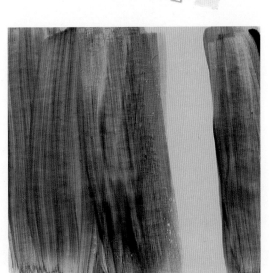

*Brush on paste tinted with burnt umber acrylic.*

*Drag with an uneven comb.*

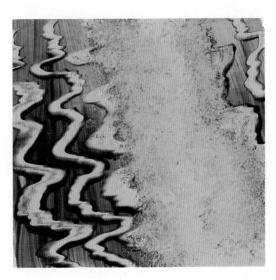

*Sponge to mottle edges.*

# DESIGNS AND VARIATIONS

There are regional variations in Bauernmalerei, although they are not all marked by country borders. Different flowers appeared in alpine and lowland designs, town-dwellers and rural farmers chose scenes that reflected their lives, and the affect of such decorative movements as Baroque or Biedermeier reached communities at varying stages. However, all Bauernmalerei celebrates simple things and pursuits in an unpretentious style.

**BAROQUE**
*With the Baroque style, flowers became more complex in colour and were given greater depth.*

spruce

light forest

crimson

brown earth

**BIRDS**
*Birds rank second to flowers in their popularity as folk art motifs.*

**SWISS SCENES**
*The Swiss were fond of representing alpine scenes, as on this design from a bucket base.*

H V,K.1823.

*burnt sienna*

*black*

### BIEDERMEIER
Painted designs were often drawn from woodwork, especially intarsia, which the spanschachtel below imitates.

*cream*  *fire red*  *forest green*

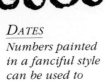

### RELIGIOUS MOTIFS
Invocations of Jesus and the virgin Mary are woven into emblems.

### DATES
Numbers painted in a fanciful style can be used to date the piece.

### BORDERS
Swiss and Austrian border designs tend to have a lighter touch.

### AUSTRIAN STYLE
This charming piece is based on an Austrian design painted in 1821.

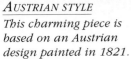

*dusty blue*

*orange*  *black*

# PROJECT: SWISS WALL CUPBOARD

If German folk art is typified by solid shapes and dark colours, Swiss design is lighter in touch. This small project bears a distinctive alpine freshness. The panel bouquet or side designs could be used independently on a box lid or clock face.

*Level of difficulty: Intermediate*

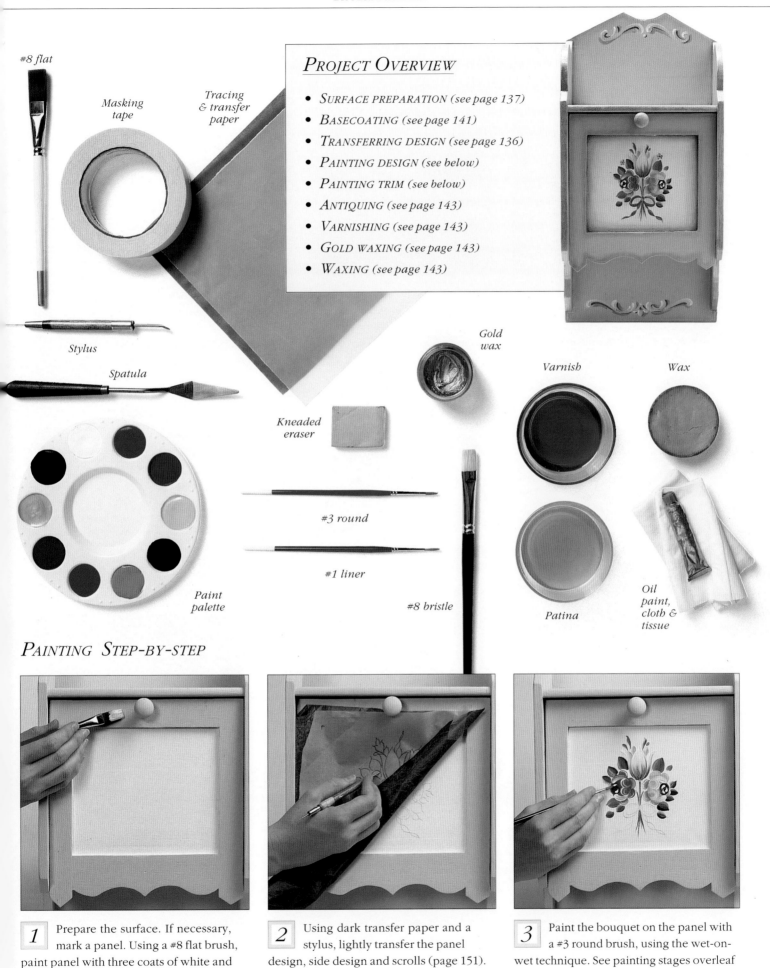

*#8 flat*

*Masking tape*

*Tracing & transfer paper*

## PROJECT OVERVIEW

- SURFACE PREPARATION (see page 137)
- BASECOATING (see page 141)
- TRANSFERRING DESIGN (see page 136)
- PAINTING DESIGN (see below)
- PAINTING TRIM (see below)
- ANTIQUING (see page 143)
- VARNISHING (see page 143)
- GOLD WAXING (see page 143)
- WAXING (see page 143)

*Stylus*

*Spatula*

*Gold wax*

*Varnish*

*Wax*

*Kneaded eraser*

*Paint palette*

*#3 round*

*#1 liner*

*#8 bristle*

*Patina*

*Oil paint, cloth & tissue*

## PAINTING STEP-BY-STEP

**1** Prepare the surface. If necessary, mark a panel. Using a #8 flat brush, paint panel with three coats of white and paint surrounds with two coats of mint.

**2** Using dark transfer paper and a stylus, lightly transfer the panel design, side design and scrolls (page 151).

**3** Paint the bouquet on the panel with a #3 round brush, using the wet-on-wet technique. See painting stages overleaf for colours and brushstrokes.

**4** Paint the scrolls above and below the panel and on the sides with a #3 round, using the wet-on-wet technique. Refer to painting stages for detail. Paint flowers on the side designs.

**5** Use a #1 liner brush to paint rust panel border and gold trim. Strengthen with a second coat. Use the #1 liner to paint gold highlight on scrolls.

**6** When dry, erase all lines. Antique lightly with raw umber oil paint and varnish. Apply gold wax to the edges of the piece with a soft cloth, then use clear wax over entire piece.

## BOUQUET PAINTING STAGES

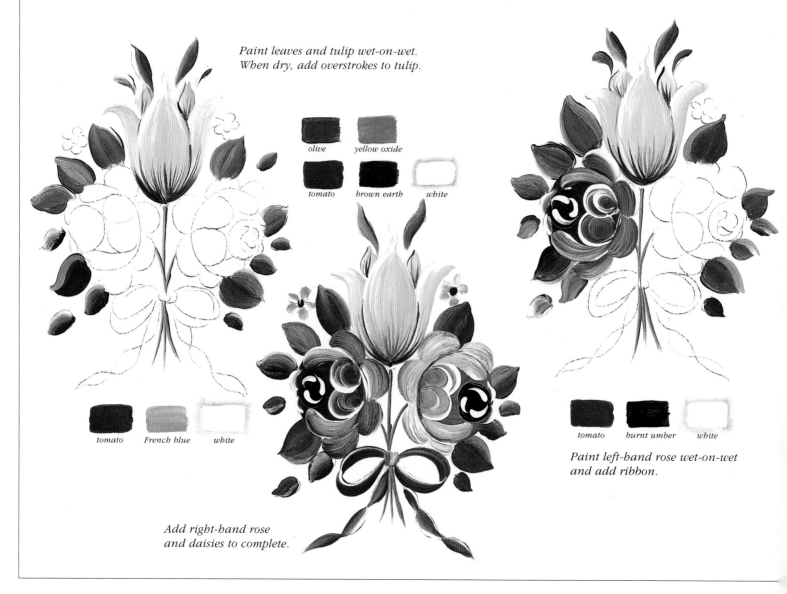

*Paint leaves and tulip wet-on-wet. When dry, add overstrokes to tulip.*

olive    yellow oxide

tomato    brown earth    white

tomato    French blue    white

*Add right-hand rose and daisies to complete.*

tomato    burnt umber    white

*Paint left-hand rose wet-on-wet and add ribbon.*

## SIDE PANEL PAINTING STAGES

Paint scrollwork
wet-on-wet.

pine     brown earth

white

Paint leaves wet-on-wet.

olive     yellow oxide

white

tomato     burnt umber     gold

French blue     white     ivory

Add flowers and wash in
a shadow to complete.

# PROJECT: AUSTRIAN CHEST OF DRAWERS

The design for this project is adapted from an Austrian pine armoire painted in 1810. Imitation woodgraining was often painted to suggest more expensive and popular timbers; here, two graining techniques are used to mimic different timbers.

*Level of difficulty: Beginner*

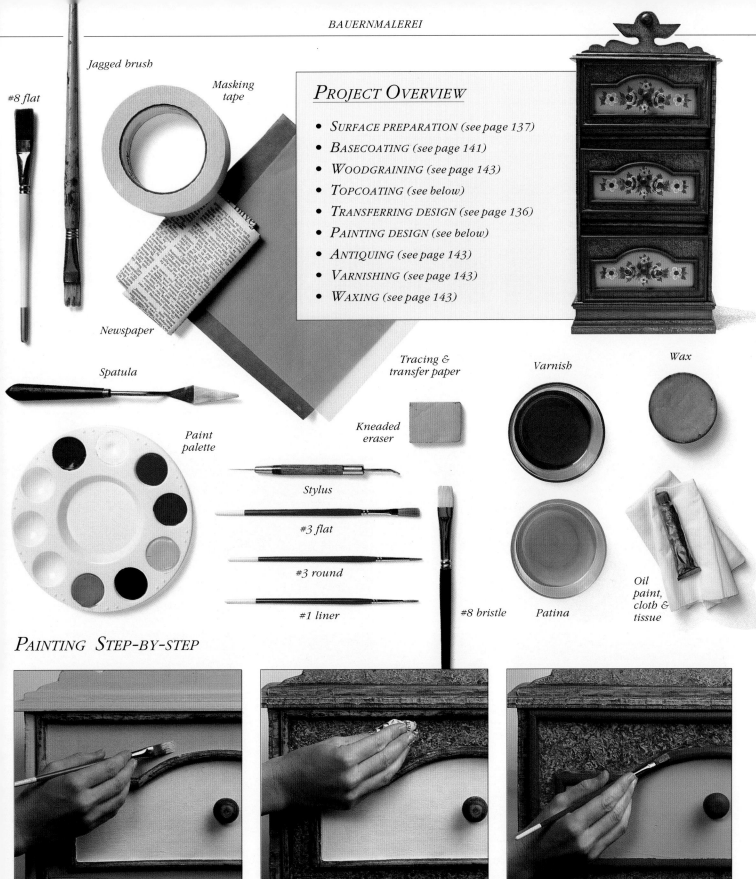

#8 flat

Jagged brush

Masking tape

## PROJECT OVERVIEW

- SURFACE PREPARATION (see page 137)
- BASECOATING (see page 141)
- WOODGRAINING (see page 143)
- TOPCOATING (see below)
- TRANSFERRING DESIGN (see page 136)
- PAINTING DESIGN (see below)
- ANTIQUING (see page 143)
- VARNISHING (see page 143)
- WAXING (see page 143)

Newspaper

Spatula

Tracing & transfer paper

Varnish

Wax

Paint palette

Kneaded eraser

Stylus

#3 flat

#3 round

#1 liner

#8 bristle

Patina

Oil paint, cloth & tissue

# PAINTING STEP-BY-STEP

**1** Prepare the surface as appropriate. If necessary, mark out panels with a ruler and pencil. Use a #8 flat brush to basecoat around the panels in pine and within the panels in white. Leave to dry.

**2** Woodgrain around the panels; refer overleaf for a detailed explanation. Use crumpled newspaper on the top of the chest and on the drawers. Use a jagged brush in a swivelling motion on the sides.

**3** Use a #8 flat brush to paint the panels dusty blue. When dry, paint the beading or borders in rust colour with a #3 flat brush.

**4** Using dark transfer paper and a stylus, transfer the designs (page 152) onto each of the drawers and onto the sides of the chest.

**5** With a #3 round brush, paint the design using the wet-on-wet technique. See painting stages below for colours and brushstrokes.

**6** Paint the white trim with a #1 liner. When dry, erase all lines, then antique, varnish and wax to complete.

## Woodgraining Painting Stages

Two woodgrain patterns appear in this project; both use the basic technique of laying down a coat of tinted paste and marking patterns with a tool. The front of the chest of drawers has been smudged with crumpled newspaper to imitate walnut. A swivelling pattern has been created on the top and sides using a jagged brush, that is, one that has been hacked at with a pair of scissors.

*Seal with paste, then paint on tinted paste.*

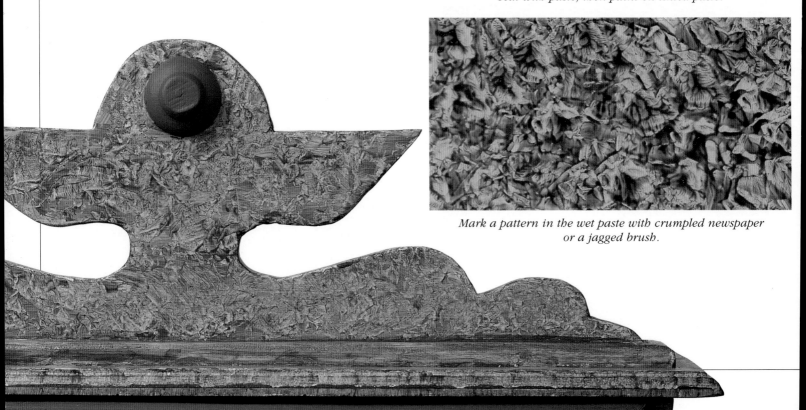

*Mark a pattern in the wet paste with crumpled newspaper or a jagged brush.*

# SIDE PANEL PAINTING STAGES

Paint leaves wet-on-wet and add stems.

Paint roses wet-on-wet.

Add daisies to complete.

| | | |
|---|---|---|
| spruce | white | |
| fire red | burnt sienna | white |

straw        white        fire red

# CLASSIC FRENCH STYLE

*FRENCH FURNITURE summons to mind beautifully carved or turned pieces, delicately painted with flowers or fruit seen through a patina of age. Whether they have the elegance of the Parisian court or the simplicity of the provinces, French pieces painted in the seventeenth and eighteenth centuries have a charm that distinguishes French style from English or German design of the same period.*

*Provincial cupboard*

The kings who reigned over France at that time were fond of displaying their wealth and had a penchant for things exotic and elaborate. Chinoiserie - the imitation of Oriental design - took a strong hold in France during this period. Potters and furniture-makers copied oriental designs and strove to simulate lacquerware. This fashion paved the way for the fanciful style known as Rococo, in which the asymmetry and motifs of chinoiserie were combined with feathery curves and subtle embellishments.

Provincial artisans imitated work done in the capital and the relative proximity of a region to Paris affected its design. Normandy, the neighbouring province, produced graceful armoires and buffets with such sculpted motifs as flower baskets or kissing doves. Brittany, further afield and more isolated, created plainer pieces decorated with marquetry or *brulage au fer*, otherwise known as pokerwork. The quality of wood available affected whether rustic decoration was carved or painted. Pine, an

*The palace of Fontainebleau, once the residence of Napoleon, is decorated in a curious mixture of styles.*

inexpensive wood, was not suitable for marquetry or sculpture and so was painted with red and green geometric patterns and rosettes. Local timbers were sometimes treated to take on the colour and patina of mahogany and ebony.

The region which is most closely identified with French provincial is Provence. Despite its distance from Paris, it was strongly affected by the styles of Louis XV and XVI. Here, however, the motifs reflected rural concerns: sheaves of wheat, olive branches, pine cones and grapes, along with the more conventional roses and shells.

The Revolution dampened the enthusiasm for ornate Rococo design, but Napoleon's victories soon inspired a taste for classical emblems and proportions. The neo-classical style called on motifs of ancient Greece and Rome, adding wreaths and anthemions to the repertoire of classic French style.

*This chinoiserie tray is an example of* tôle peinte *or japanned tinware.*

# DESIGNS AND VARIATIONS

There is really no single French style. French design can play with understatement or overindulge in detail. It can dip into rustic traditions or explore the motifs of a particular period. Decorative painters can choose between various provincial styles, the ornate Rococo or the Napoleonic grandeur of neo-classical, and still produce something that is classic French.

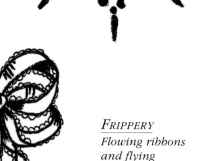

**SOURCES**
*Fabrics offer a wonderful source of inspiration for French design.*

**FRIPPERY**
*Flowing ribbons and flying cherubs add a touch of excess.*

**BORDERS**
*Provincial motifs such as small flowers or wheat sprays can be repeated quickly and easily.*

**FLORALS**
*An antique tapestry cartoon inspires with an array of blossoms.*

*olive*

*dark olive*

*crimson*

54

## FLEUR-DE-LYS
*The classic iris or lily motif has its origins in medieval France.*

*crimson*

*burnt umber*

## CARVINGS
*Rosettes and sheaves of wheat were carved and painted on rustic furniture.*

*oatmeal*

*black wash*

*white*

## GILDED-GREY
*This arch reflects the restrained tastes of the Directoire period, 1795-1799.*

## NEOCLASSICAL
*The anthemion, a stylized honeysuckle, is one of the motifs recovered from ancient Greece.*

## FOLIAGE
*Vine leaves, olive branches and acorns were popular subjects in the Provence region.*

55

# PROJECT: FRENCH TABLE AND CHAIR

The Rococo style is characterized by light patterns, pastel colours and delicate proportions: all three meet in this classic rose design. The graceful cabriole legs on these two pieces are also a feature of furniture from that period.

*Level of difficulty: Intermediate*

asecoater

*Masking tape*

*Crackle medium*

#8 bristle

*Spatula*

*Tracing & transfer paper*

*Kneaded eraser*

*Stylus*

*#6 flat*

*#3 flat*

*#3 round*

*#1 liner*

*Paint palette*

*Gold wax*

*Varnish*

*Wax*

*Sea sponge*

*Patina*

*Oil paint, cloth & tissue*

## PROJECT OVERVIEW

- SURFACE PREPARATION (see page 137)
- BASECOATING (see page 141)
- APPLYING CRACKLE (see page 142)
- TOPCOATING (see below)
- TRANSFERRING DESIGN (see page 136)
- PAINTING DESIGN (see below)
- WASHING (see below)
- ANTIQUING (see page 143)
- VARNISHING (see page 143)
- GOLD WAXING (see page 143)

## PAINTING STEP-BY-STEP

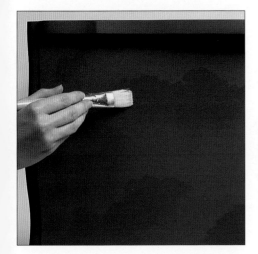

*1* Prepare the surface as appropriate. Basecoat with rust colour. With a #8 bristle brush, paint patches of crackle medium; avoid areas where the design will be painted.

*2* When the crackle medium is almost dry, lightly sponge on a cream topcoat. Continue sponging the entire surface lightly with paint to create a mottled effect and then leave to dry.

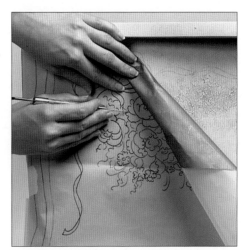

*3* Using dark transfer paper and a stylus, lightly transfer the designs (page 152-3). There are two for the top of the table and one which can be used on both sides of the chair back.

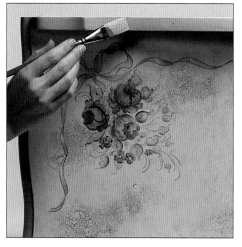

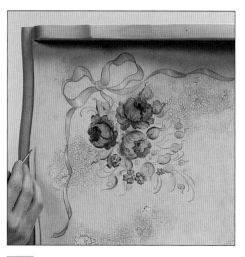

*4* To paint the designs, wash in base colours with a #3 flat, float shadows and highlights with a #3 round, and add detail with a #1 liner. See painting stages below. When dry, erase all lines.

*5* Use a #6 flat brush to paint a mint-coloured wash around the edges of the table. For treatment of the cabriole legs, see the illustrations opposite.

*6* Add a gold trim line with a #1 liner. When dry, antique lightly with raw umber oil paint and then varnish. Apply gold wax to highlight edges and then apply clear wax to entire piece.

## CHAIR DESIGN PAINTING STAGES

*Note: all colours are washes.*

*Wash in ribbon.*

*Float leaves and shadow on ribbon.*

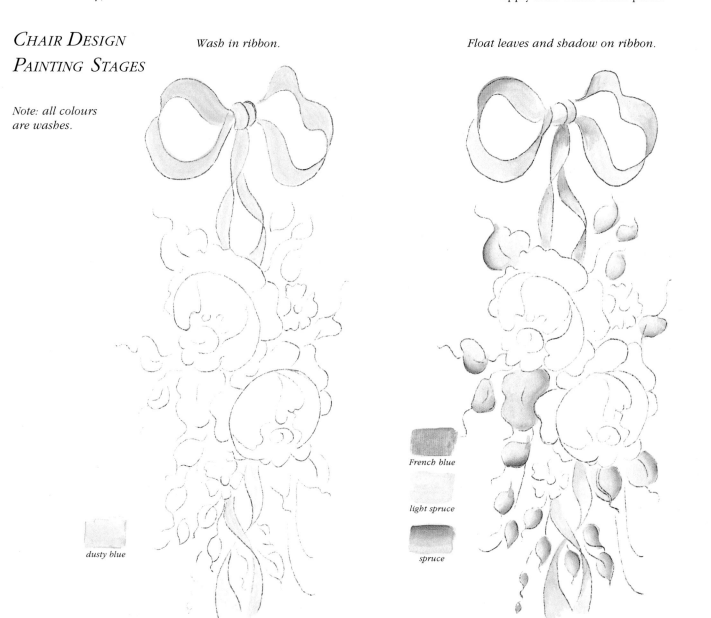

*French blue*

*light spruce*

*spruce*

*dusty blue*

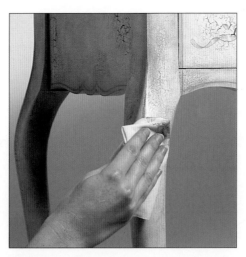

**7** Highlight the curve of the cabriole leg by lightly sponging with a mint-coloured wash.

**8** After varnishing the entire piece, apply gold wax to accentuate the curve further.

*Wash in roses and float highlights.*

*Paint shadows on roses. Add daisies and linework to complete.*

*brown*

*light peach*

*salmon*

*peach*

*dark peach*

*brown*

*dusty blue*

*French blue*

*salmon*

*white*

# PROJECT: ROCOCO JEWELLERY BOX

The term Rococo is derived from the French word *rocaille* meaning 'shell'. This box features a shell with elaborate scrolls, as well as a delicate floral arrangement which owes much to chinoiserie. Paint the inside of the box or line it with fabric to complete the project.

*Level of difficulty: Intermediate*

Basecoater

Masking tape

Crackle medium

Sea sponge

#8 flat

Spatula

Paint palette

Tracing & transfer paper

Stylus

#6 flat

#3 round

#1 liner

#8 bristle

Kneaded eraser

Varnish

Wax

Patina

Oil paint, cloth & tissue

## PROJECT OVERVIEW

- SURFACE PREPARATION (see page 137)
- BASECOATING (see page 141)
- APPLYING CRACKLE (see page 142)
- TOPCOATING (see below)
- TRANSFER DESIGN (see page 136)
- PAINTING DESIGN (see below)
- SELECTIVE ANTIQUING (see below)
- GENERAL ANTIQUING (see page 143)
- VARNISHING (see page 143)
- WAXING (see page 143)

## PAINTING STEP-BY-STEP

**1** Prepare the surface. Basecoat in rust. When dry, use a #8 flat brush to paint patches of crackle medium. When crackle medium is almost dry, sponge white paint over the patches.

**2** Topcoat the remainder of the box white using a #6 flat brush. Recoat three times, each time avoiding the crackled areas. Leave to dry.

**3** Paint the box with a yellow wash using a #6 flat. Leave to dry. Using transfer paper and a stylus, lightly transfer the designs (page 154-5). Basecoat flowers and ribbon white, using a #3 round.

4   Paint the floral design, using a #3 round brush for base colours and floatwork and a #1 liner for detail. Refer to the floral painting stages for colours and brushstrokes.

5   Paint the scrolls and shell, using a #3 round for the wash and floatwork and a #1 liner for detail. Refer to the painting stages below for colours. When dry, erase all lines.

6   Antique edges and corners with raw umber oil paint and allow to dry. Antique generally with raw sienna, taking care to avoid the ribbon. Varnish and wax to complete.

## ROCAILLE PAINTING STAGES

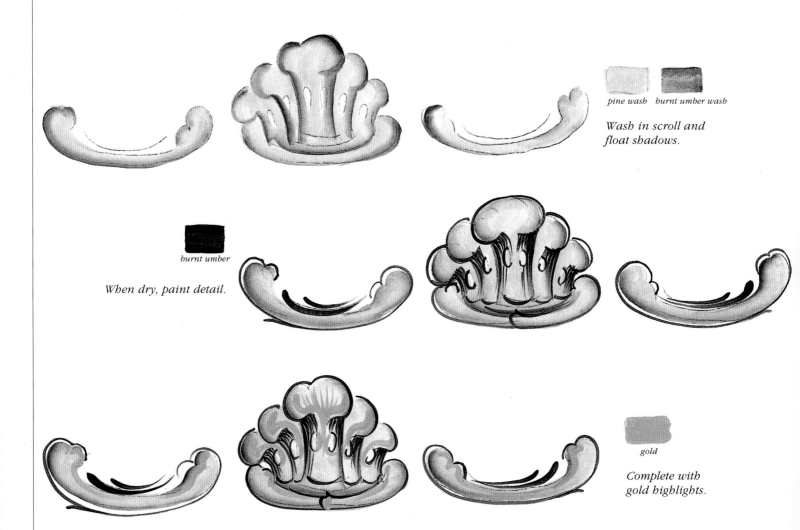

*pine wash*    *burnt umber wash*

*Wash in scroll and float shadows.*

*burnt umber*

*When dry, paint detail.*

*gold*

*Complete with gold highlights.*

# FLORAL PAINTING STAGES

*Note: all colours are washes.*

olive

burnt sienna

*Wash leaves in green and float a highlight.*

raw sienna   peach

grape   dusty blue

*Add rose, tulip, poppies and daisies.*

burnt umber

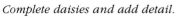

raw sienna   red

*Complete daisies and add detail.*

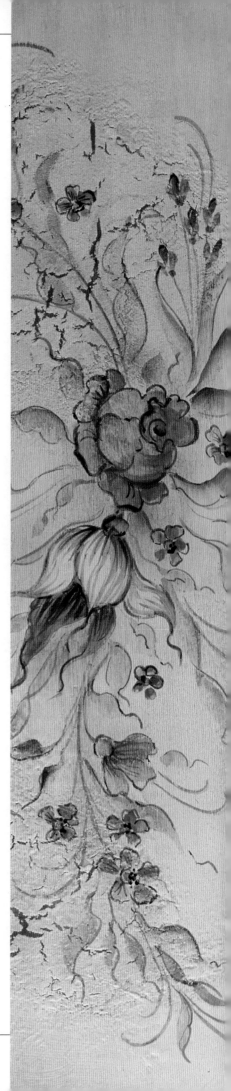

# FOLK PAINTING
# OF SWEDEN

*Sweden's monarch in the 1770s was Gustavus III, a man of culture who set the standard for which Swedish design is now renowned. The folk artists of his country simplified Gustavian neoclassicism, but kept the clean lines and delicate palette to produce a style that is fresh and appealing.*

The central district of Dalarna was a stronghold for decorative painting. This farming region, which includes the towns of Mora, Leksand, Rattvik, Falun and Borlange, gained a reputation for its travelling painters, who used linework and strokes to define the flowers and leaves, instead of the delicate shading used by the Norwegians. These folk artists received small commissions for painting pieces of furniture: clocks, large cabinets, doors of bed chambers and room panels. The latter were painted on to cloth or on heavy paper which was then attached to the wall.

*Mora clock*

Many of the scenes depicted in the wall paintings were biblical in theme but the figures wore the local dress of the time and biblical towns were depicted as present-day Swedish towns, offering a picture book of the scriptures for those unable to read. Special events in the

*A series of wall panels adds interest to an otherwise plain room; the rustic furniture reflects the orange and blue tones.*

community, such as weddings or baptisms, were represented and sometimes the artist added a portrait of the peasants who had commissioned the work, with an inscription noting some quaint detail of their lives.

Most designs feature a kurbits: a floral spray or vine that arches over the scene or sprouts out of an urn or a building. Each kurbits is made up of large leaves, a middle flower, side flowers, stamens and swirling tendrils. The original kurbits was a gift of the Lord to Jonah, intended to provide shelter and comfort, but to the Swedish countryfolk it also represented fertility.

Another motif from the Dalarna area is the Dala horse, a carved figure painted red or blue. Today, one cannot visit Sweden without seeing hundreds of these brightly painted horses in many sizes. Together with kurbits and wall scenes they have become known as the signatures of Sweden.

*This panel, complete with kurbits, probably depicts a biblical scene.*

# DESIGNS AND VARIATIONS

The light colours of Gustavian style greatly affected the palette of Swedish folk painting, leaving a preference for creams and siennas and for washes rather than solid or blended colours. In addition, sharp outlining of figures and motifs contributes to a cleanness of design.

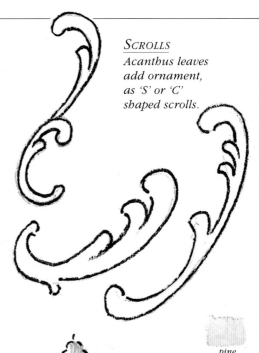

### SCROLLS
*Acanthus leaves add ornament, as 'S' or 'C' shaped scrolls.*

### WOODGRAINING
*A false grain has been painted over an old design on this chest.*

*pine*

*raw sienna*

*white*

### CARVINGS
*Simple but classic patterns can be drawn from carved furniture.*

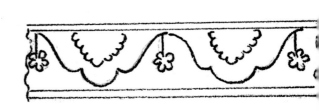

### FLOWERS
*Blossoms tend to be stylized and simplified.*

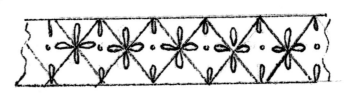

### BORDERS
*Small elements are arranged to create detailed strips of pattern.*

*peach*

*pine*

*Prussian blue*

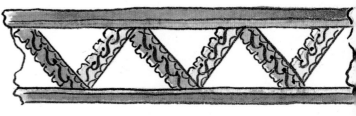

### KURBITS
The tree of life can spring from anywhere and often dominates the design.

olive    Prussian blue

pimento

### FIGURES
No Swedish wall painting is complete without a Dala horse, preferably blue.

### SCENES
Stylized buildings and trees usually form the backdrop for a procession.

pine

Prussian blue

pimento

olive

# Project: Swedish Chair

A plain chair is given much grace with a kurbits motif, modified and repeated. Raw pine furniture is inexpensive and, once pickled, beautifully conveys the fresh Swedish style. This project also demonstrates the process of selective antiquing.

*Level of difficulty: Beginner*

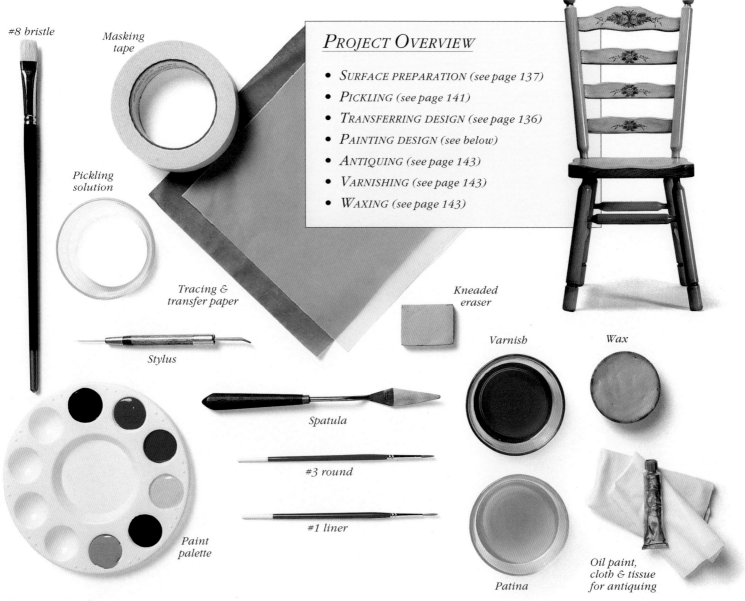

#8 bristle

Masking
tape

Pickling
solution

**PROJECT OVERVIEW**

- SURFACE PREPARATION *(see page 137)*
- PICKLING *(see page 141)*
- TRANSFERRING DESIGN *(see page 136)*
- PAINTING DESIGN *(see below)*
- ANTIQUING *(see page 143)*
- VARNISHING *(see page 143)*
- WAXING *(see page 143)*

Tracing &
transfer paper

Kneaded
eraser

Stylus

Varnish

Wax

Spatula

#3 round

#1 liner

Paint
palette

Patina

Oil paint,
cloth & tissue
for antiquing

## PAINTING STEP-BY-STEP

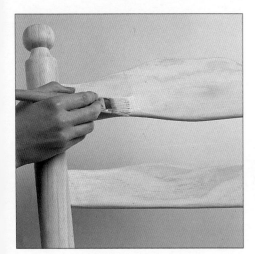

*1* Prepare the surface if using an old piece. Dampen the raw wood slightly with a cloth. Using a #8 bristle brush, paint on the pickling solution. Apply a second coat and leave to dry.

*2* Transfer the designs (page 155). Be careful not to press too heavily with the stylus or the lines of the design will show through the paintwork.

*3* Refer to the kurbits painting stages overleaf for colours and brush-strokes. Use a #3 round brush to paint the large leaves with an olive wash.

**4** Using a #3 round brush, partially wash in the orange flowers so that wood shows through sections of the petals.

**5** Use the #3 round brush to paint small leaves with a Prussian blue wash.

**6** Detail in charcoal with a #1 liner. When dry, erase design lines. Antique the chair, emphasizing the contours. Varnish and wax to complete.

## KURBITS PAINTING STAGES

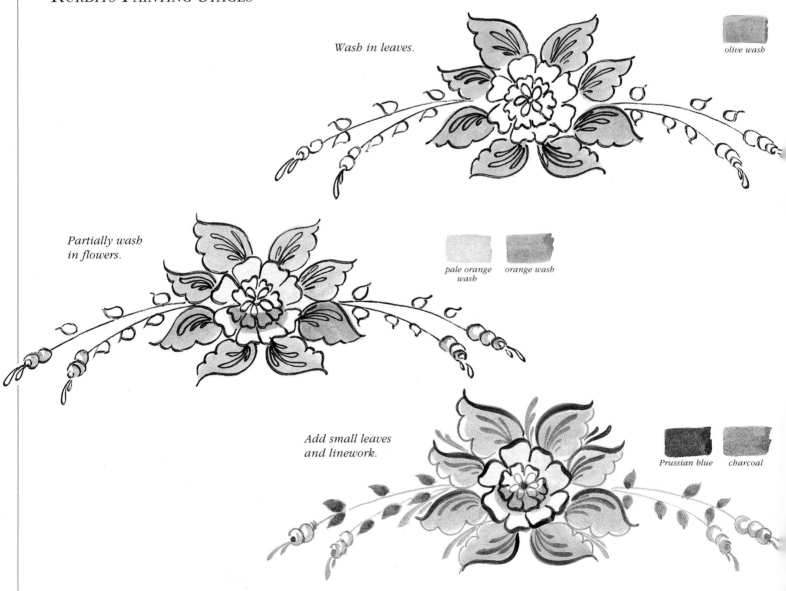

*Wash in leaves.*

*olive wash*

*Partially wash in flowers.*

*pale orange wash*   *orange wash*

*Add small leaves and linework.*

*Prussian blue*   *charcoal*

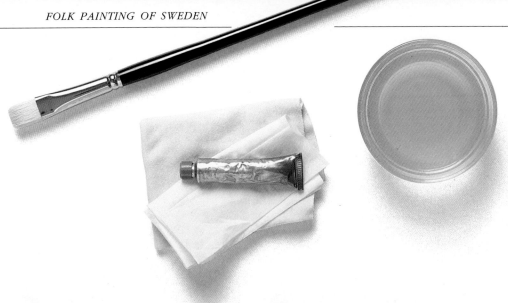

## ANTIQUING PAINTING STAGES

Adding a patina of age tones down the colours of a design and adds dimension and charm to a finished piece. Concentrate on areas which would be most worn, and on cracks and grooves where grime would collect over time. You can also create shadows which will focus the eye on the design area. In this project, the ends of each slat have been given attention, as well as the chair seat.

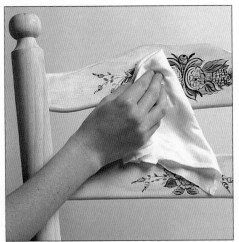

1 Lightly rub patina on to the wood with a soft cloth.

2 Using a #8 bristle brush, paint burnt umber oil paint on to selected areas.

3 Remove excess paint with a tissue. Blend the remaining paint with a soft cloth.

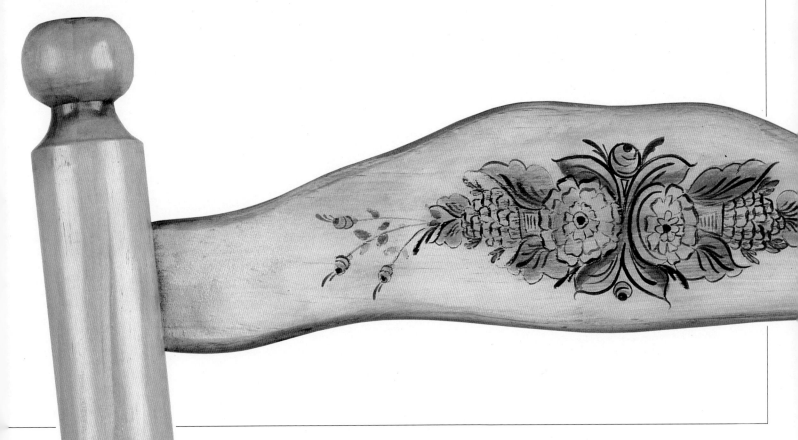

# PROJECT: SCANDINAVIAN WRITING BUREAU

This design reflects the taste of the Swedish nobility for decorating furniture in the style of the French court, however the soft grey-blue wash gives it a strong Scandinavian flavour. The delicate floatwork requires some practice.

*Level of difficulty: Advanced*

Ruler

Masking
tape

Basecoater

Openweave
cloth

## PROJECT OVERVIEW

- SURFACE PREPARATION (see page 137)
- BASECOATING (see page 141)
- ADDING PANEL (see below)
- DISTRESSING (see page 142)
- WASHING AROUND PANEL (see below)
- TRANSFERRING DESIGN (see page 136)
- PAINTING DESIGN (see below)
- ANTIQUING (see page 143)
- VARNISHING (see page 143)
- GOLD WAXING (see page 143)
- WAXING (see page 143)

Pencil

Wet-&-dry

#8 flat

Stylus

Tracing
& transfer
paper

Kneaded
eraser

Varnish

Gold
& clear
wax

Paint
palette

Spatula

#6 flat

#3 flat

#3 round

#1 liner

#8 bristle

Patina

Oil
paint,
cloth &
tissue

## PAINTING STEP-BY-STEP

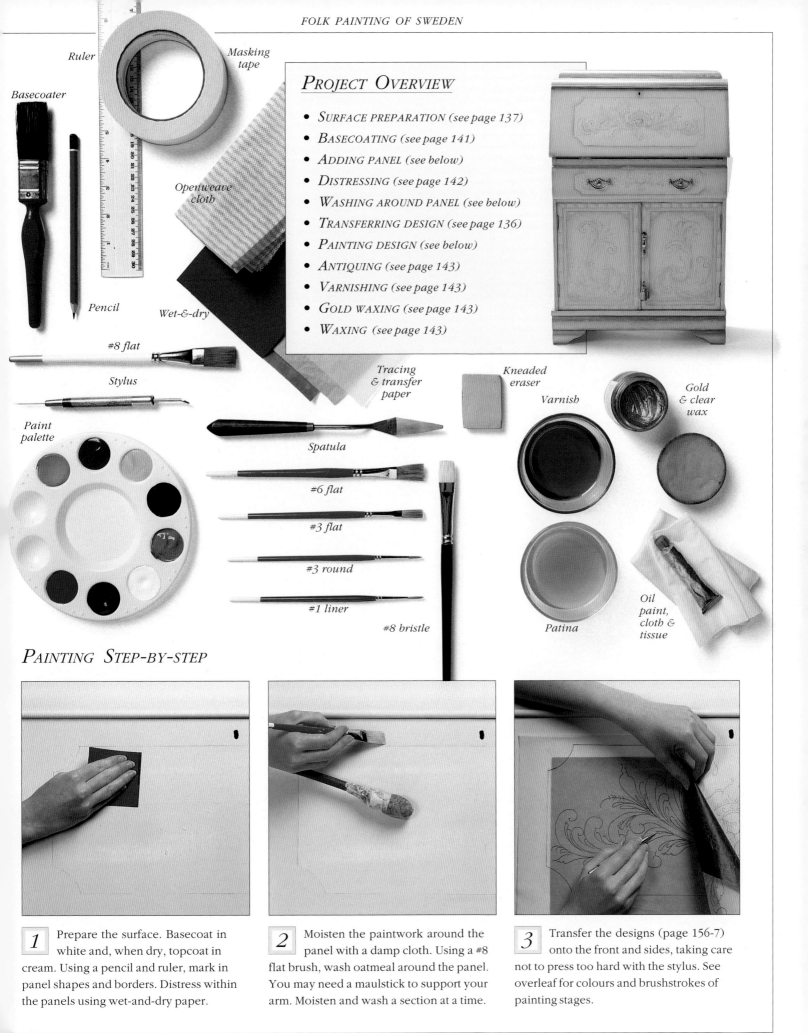

*1* Prepare the surface. Basecoat in white and, when dry, topcoat in cream. Using a pencil and ruler, mark in panel shapes and borders. Distress within the panels using wet-and-dry paper.

*2* Moisten the paintwork around the panel with a damp cloth. Using a #8 flat brush, wash oatmeal around the panel. You may need a maulstick to support your arm. Moisten and wash a section at a time.

*3* Transfer the designs (page 156-7) onto the front and sides, taking care not to press too hard with the stylus. See overleaf for colours and brushstrokes of painting stages.

*4*    Paint design as indicated below. Use a #3 flat to float scrolls and a #3 round to paint flowers. Add highlight and linework with a #1 liner.

*5*    Side-load a #6 flat brush with a mixture of oatmeal and grey and paint a wash of this mixture in a shadow around the panel to add depth.

*6*    Paint gold trim around panel with a #1 liner. Distress designs lightly. Erase lines, antique and varnish. Apply gold wax selectively and wax clear.

## SCROLLWORK PAINTING STAGES

*Float main scrolls.*

*grey*

*Float remaining scrolls and leaves. Add linework to grey areas.*

*cream*

*Prussian blue wash*

*Add linework to cream areas and highlight with gold.*

*raw sienna*

*gold*

# FLOWER PAINTING STAGES

*Wash in flower.*

*pine wash*

*Add detail.*

*raw sienna wash*

*Paint highlight.*

*gold*

*Float a shadow.*

*grey wash*

# PAINTING THE BORDER

**1** Use a #6 flat to float oatmeal-grey on the door to create a false beading. Paint the gold trim line with a #1 liner.

**2** Paint gold strokes at intervals along the border with a #3 round. Use a #1 liner to pull fine lines from each stroke.

# NORWEGIAN ROSEMALING

*ROSEMALING, or 'rose painting', is the name given to the Norwegian rustic painting of the eighteenth and nineteenth centuries. Roses—together with the acanthus scroll—were the most important elements of Norwegian folk art, the roots of which lie in the elaborate carved scrolls found on Viking longboats.*

*Telemark bowl*

Rosemaling was introduced in rural homes on small objects: ale bowls, tankards and the prized dowry chest. These gave colour to the otherwise plain interiors where families spent long dark winters. Early homes were poorly ventilated; so much soot covered the walls and furnishings that decoration was reserved for festival days. The arrival of the fireplace with an attached chimney made it feasible to display decorations the year around. Entire rooms were covered in rosemaling, geometrics and feathering on walls, cupboards, ceilings and furniture. Rosemalers sometimes added biblical and wedding scenes painted in a primitive style, in sharp contrast to the sophisticated flower painting.

Norway's mountainous terrain isolated various regions, resulting in three distinct styles of rosemaling.

*The interior of many Norwegian homes bore carved panelling, heavily decorated with rosemaling.*

*Dowry chest dated 1808*

The Hallingdal valley in central Norway produced a Baroque style characterized by strong symmetrical designs and bold hues. Rosemaling in the Telemark area, influenced by the Rococo style, is flowing and asymmetrical with intricate shading and linework. Many Telemark painters used a transparent technique on the background, allowing the woodgrain to show; others preferred black, red and white as background colours. The Rogaland style developed on the southwest coast where trading vessels brought Oriental influences, such as dark backgrounds and delicate cross-hatching. Tulips and other flowers were painted with a degree of realism and light and dark colours were used as contrasts. In each of these painting traditions, design elements were arranged quite differently.

*Hallingdal cupboard*

All rosemaling is strokework painting at its finest. The artist must first master the 'C' and 'S' strokes that comprise the scrolls. The design is then enhanced with commas, teardrops, long delicate lines and detailing in a single colour which ties the design together.

# DESIGNS AND VARIATIONS

Flowers, scrolls and more flowers make up the subject matter of the rosemaler's work. Regional variations affect the degree of symmetry and whether the flower or the scrollwork dominates, but all rosemaling is characterized by a bold use of earthy colours and a confident brushstroke.

*French blue*

*pine*

*burnt umber*

### TELEMARK
*This food box shows the transparent technique popular in the Telemark region.*

### FLOWERS
*Roses are painted from different perspectives, but usually with billowing petals.*

### COLOURS
*A Norwegian weaving shows the full-bodied Hallingdal colours.*

*rust*   *raw sienna*   *black*   *white*

## C-STROKES
Practise painting
unadorned C-strokes
until you are confident.

## ACANTHUS
The thorns of the
foliage become
decorative elements.

Prussian blue    French blue

pale blue    white

burnt sienna

raw sienna

brown

## FLOATWORK
Carefully blended
colours characterize
all rosemaling.

## SCRIPT
Paint fine
script with a
#1 liner.

*ABCD*

*Anno*
*1850*

## BORDERS
Borders are kept
simple, allowing
the main design to
dominate.

Prussian blue    raw sienna

French blue    white

# PROJECT: ROSEMALING BENCH

Exuberant patterns, intense colours and skilled floatwork
are all hallmarks of rosemaling. The inscription on the
top of this bench reads "Good health and spirits;
welcome and sit down".

*Level of difficulty: Advanced*

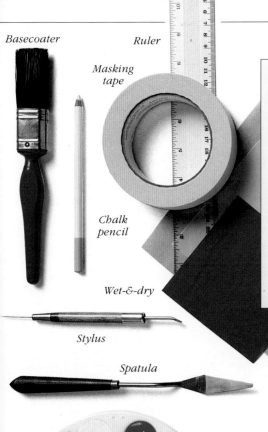

Basecoater

Ruler

Masking tape

Chalk pencil

Wet-&-dry

Stylus

Spatula

## PROJECT OVERVIEW

- SURFACE PREPARATION (see page 137)
- BASECOATING (see page 141)
- PAINTING PANELS (see below)
- DISTRESSING (see page 142)
- TRANSFERRING DESIGN (see page 136)
- PAINTING DESIGN (see below)
- ANTIQUING (see page 143)
- VARNISHING (see page 143)
- WAXING (see page 143)

Tracing & transfer paper

Kneaded eraser

Varnish

Wax

#8 flat

#3 flat

#3 round

#1 liner

Paint palette

#8 bristle

Oil paint, cloth & tissue

Patina

## PAINTING STEP-BY-STEP

**1** Prepare the surface. Basecoat rust. Use a chalk pencil and ruler to mark panels as appropriate and paint panels French blue with a #8 flat. When dry, distress panels with wet-and-dry paper.

**2** Transfer the designs (page 158-9) onto the top, sides and legs using light-coloured transfer paper.

**3** See painting stages overleaf for colours and strokes. Paint wet-on-wet, a section at a time. Use a #3 flat for painting the main strokes, and for shading. Use a #3 round for smaller comma strokes.

4   Add overstrokes and other detail with a #1 liner. Using a #3 flat brush, paint two coats of cream in a border as shown in Step 5. While paint is still wet, continue with the next step.

5   Use a #1 liner to paint a series of Prussian blue crescents at intervals around the border, then pull out fine lines from the crescent. Paint a rust crescent beside each blue one.

6   Use a #3 round brush with a fine point to paint the rust lettering. Leave to dry, erase the lines of the design and then antique. Varnish and wax to complete.

## FLOWER PAINTING STAGES

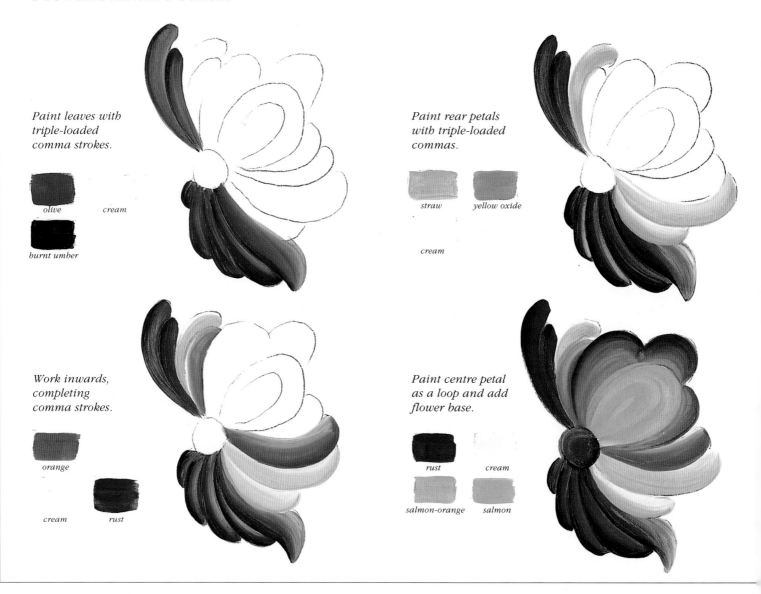

*Paint leaves with triple-loaded comma strokes.*

olive     cream

burnt umber

*Paint rear petals with triple-loaded commas.*

straw     yellow oxide

cream

*Work inwards, completing comma strokes.*

orange

cream     rust

*Paint centre petal as a loop and add flower base.*

rust     cream

salmon-orange     salmon

## SCROLL PAINTING STAGES

*Paint main stroke and then overstroke with a side-loaded brush.*

rust  burnt umber  cream  French blue

Prussian blue

*Add large comma strokes.*

olive  salmon

*Complete and add linework.*

straw  cream  burnt umber

# HINDELOOPEN OF THE NETHERLANDS

*In the Netherlands, a history of trade with distant cultures produced a unique painting tradition that borrows decorative elements of both the West and East. Hindelooper art is unusually complex in design and combines colours to produce a strange and dramatic effect.*

*Traditional butte*

From the fifteenth to the eighteenth centuries, the town of Hindeloopen in Friesland was an important base for ships trading around the world. Much of this trade was in wooden objects and woodcarving was a local craft popular among the sailors. The painting of these carvings led naturally to painting on the furniture, doors and interior walls of Dutch homes. These early efforts were influenced by the Norwegian painting styles, but whatever Hindeloopen once owed to the Norwegian rosemalers, it quickly developed its own set of characteristics.

When the East India Company was founded in 1602, much of the Hindelooper fleet sailed for Japan, India, China and Indonesia. Dutch sailors brought home many objects of Eastern art, such as Chinese porcelain and heavily decorated fabrics known as chintz. The designs of chintz greatly influenced the basic style of Hindeloopen, with its rich, dark backgrounds and intricate detail. Hindelooper artists also attempted to imitate Chinese porcelain by painting designs in a single colour, such as blue, on an off-white background. By custom, this technique was used to decorate wedding gifts. A third variation appeared: the use of a dark blue background to signify mourning. Household objects were repainted in this sombre colour scheme for the duration of the mourning period, which traditionally lasted seven years.

In each of these stylistic variations, motifs were painted using three colours or shades: a main colour, a shadow colour and a highlight, which combined to emphasize the detail of the design. To provide some visual relief, Hindelooper artists made good use of false marbling techniques and often added biblical scenes or landscapes in a cartouche or panel. It is the striking colours and the graceful wave lines of the basic pattern, however, that sum up the Hindelooper style and best convey the unusual blend of Western and Eastern influences.

*These well worn clogs have been painted in the red-brown colour of basic Hindeloopen.*

*Cooking pot painted in mourning colour scheme*

# DESIGNS AND VARIATIONS

Hindelooper designs are a graceful mass of acanthus scrolls and small flowers and often feature a lucky bird perched among the flowers. There is little attention to proportion; the bird is a relatively small motif, while whole landscapes are happily painted within the confines of a garland. Favoured flowers include daisies, poppy heads, roses, chrysanthemums and tulips.

tomato

red oxide    ivory

### FLOWERS
*Wild roses are often painted front on, using contrasting overstrokes on a hollow circle of colour.*

### SHADES
*The use of several shades in one colour is just one of the Hindelooper colour schemes.*

dusty blue

Prussian blue

### SCENES
*Landscapes can be added in a cartouche, as on this coal scuttle.*

### PATTERNS
*A basic floral spray can be adapted to fit various panels.*

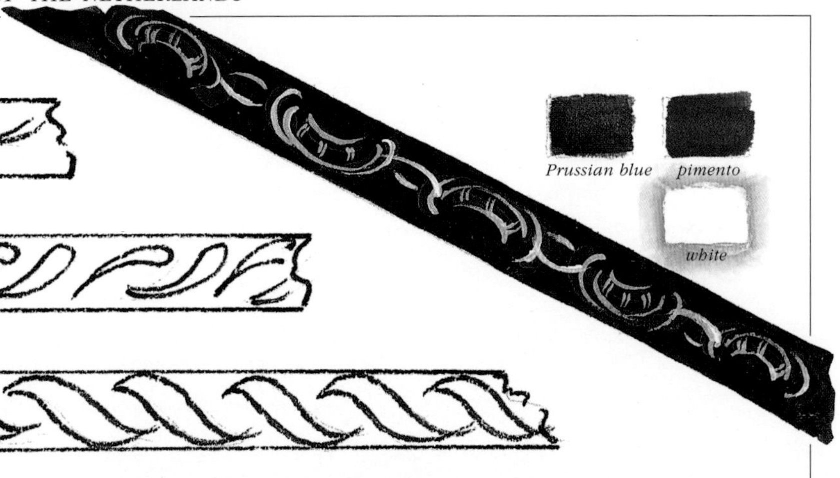

## BORDERS

Most compositions are bordered with a wave line, painted in cream or yellow-gold.

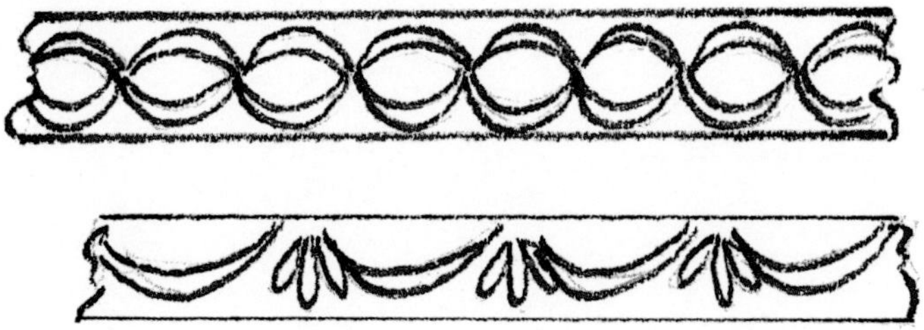

Prussian blue  pimento

white

## SCROLLS

The basic scroll can be combined in a contra form, running form or boat shape.

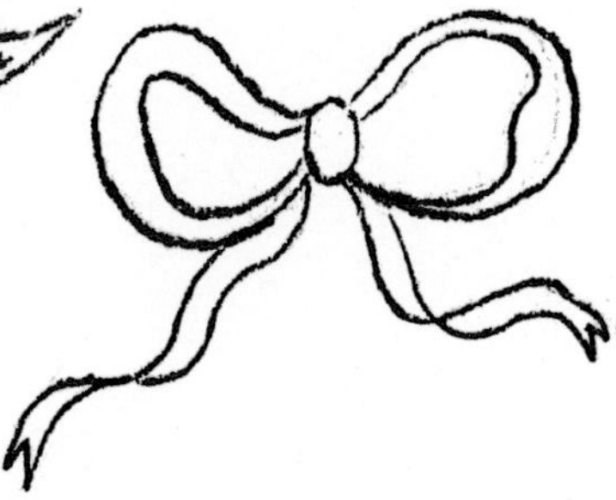

Prussian blue

pimento

ivory

## BACKGROUNDS

Green, red, dark blue and white are the basic background colours.

## BIRDS

The lucky bird is painted looking over his shoulder to keep evil spirits away.

raw sienna

pimento

Prussian blue

# PROJECT: HINDELOOPEN BUTTE

This butte, or food box, is decorated in the basic Hindeloopen
style with a strong red background and marbled trim. Hindelooper
artists paint freehand, sketching loosely in chalk, however
beginners may prefer to trace the design.

*Level of difficulty: Intermediate*

*Basecoater*  *Ruler*
*Masking tape*

*Chalk pencil*

*Stylus*

*Spatula*

*Plastic wrap*

*Tracing & transfer paper*

*Retarder*

*Kneaded eraser*

*Varnish*  *Wax*

| PROJECT OVERVIEW |
|---|

- SURFACE PREPARATION (see page 137)
- BASECOATING (see page 141)
- MARBLING BORDER (see overleaf)
- TRANSFERRING DESIGN (see page 136)
- PAINTING DESIGN (see below)
- ANTIQUING (see page 143)
- VARNISHING (see page 143)
- WAXING (see page 143)

*Paint palette*

*#6 flat*

*#3 round*

*#1 liner*

*#8 bristle*

*Patina*

*Oil paint, cloth & tissue*

# PAINTING STEP-BY-STEP

**1** Prepare the surface and basecoat in tomato. Using a pencil and ruler, mark in the border. Apply masking tape along the pencil line and, using a #6 flat brush, paint the exposed border and handle Prussian blue.

**2** When the Prussian blue paint is dry, marble the border and handle as shown overleaf. Leave to dry. Transfer the designs (page 160-1) onto the base and lid. Note that only half of the lid design has been included.

**3** Refer to painting stages overleaf for colours and brushstrokes. Use a #3 round to block in scrolls, flowers and bird and to paint overstrokes. Detail with a #1 liner. When dry, erase lines then antique, varnish and wax.

## LUCKY BIRD PAINTING STAGES

*Paint in scrollwork.*

*pimento*    *Prussian blue*

*yellow oxide*    *burnt umber*

*Add foliage, flowers and bird.*

*pimento*    *Prussian blue*

*yellow oxide*    *burnt umber*

*Add linework.*

*ivory*    *straw*

# MARBLING

For almost as long as marble has been quarried, decorative artists have imitated the veins and fractures of this symbol of wealth. In France, where it is known as *faux marbre*, the results were often convincing. Among the rural Dutch, the false finish was painted with less attention to accuracy.

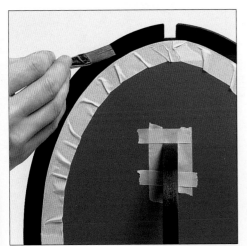

**1** Use a #6 flat brush to paint retarder medium onto the marbling areas. Move quickly on to the next step.

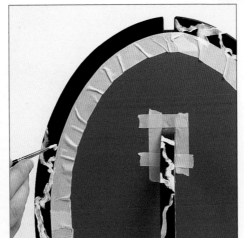

**2** While the retarder is still damp, paint random white lines on the marbling area with a #3 round brush. Again, move quickly on to the next step.

**3** Before the white lines dry, smudge them with crumpled plastic wrap, changing the angle at which the wrap is dabbed so that the pattern is varied.

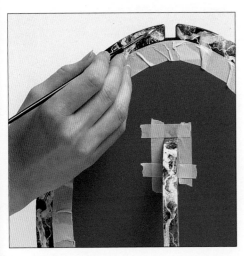

**4** Use a #1 liner to add fine white lines to represent the veins in marble.

# AMERICAN COUNTRY PAINTING

*COLONIAL AMERICA was populated by various ethnic groups, each of which brought a rich cultural heritage and a wealth of skills. The Germanic people who settled the fertile valleys of Pennsylvania in the seventeenth century had a strong painting tradition which they adapted to create a simple, fresh style.*

*Naïve houses*

The Pennsylvania Dutch, the 'Dutch' being a misnomer for 'Deutsch', worked hard and led simple lives. Events such as births, marriages and funerals were community occasions which were commemorated in *frakturs*, dower chests and mourning pictures. Regional variations in their folk art arose due to religious differences: Lutherans, who enjoyed colour and decoration, decorated their barns with large hex signs; the Amish and other 'Plain Dutch' sects shunned such worldliness.

Frakturs, a beautiful and unique form of Pennsylvanian folk art, were profusely decorated records of births, baptisms, marriages, and houseblessings drawn in inks on laid paper and coloured with watercolours or vegetable dyes. Fraktur lettering, or Frakturschrift, was in gothic German and often expressed a biblical sentiment. The decorated dower chest was a traditional part of a bride's dowry. Given to her by her father, she brought it to her new home filled with linens she had spun and embroidered. Often the owner's name and the year it was made were incorporated into the decoration. The bride box was usually a gift from the bridegroom, in which the bride saved her wedding veil and other small treasures. Similar to a bonnet box in size and shape, it usually depicted the bride and groom on the lid with a sentimental inscription. In the late eighteenth century, such household articles as coffee pots, trays, boxes and canisters were made of

*Deutsch box*

tinplate and, when japanning became popular, gaily painted with bold stroke designs.

Pennsylvania Dutch painting is less ornate than its European origins. Motifs are simple and colours bright and bold: two characteristics of American country painting in general. Indeed, Pennsylvania Dutch style has become almost synonymous with American folk art.

*Brightly painted whirligigs are a trademark of the American country style.*

*This chest is painted in the traditional Pennsylvanian blue.*

# DESIGNS AND VARIATIONS

American decorative painting conveys a sense that anything is possible. Unicorns and mermaids, angels and brave horsemen, symbolizing purity of heart and spirit, feature boldly among stars and flowers. Farm animals are painted as if they have a special place in art and colour combinations are dramatic if not gaudy.

### PRIMITIVE
*Naively painted figures and animals have become a favourite aspect of American country style.*

### COLOURS
*Peacock plumage offers an excuse for bright colours.*

*straw*

*peach*

*dusty blue*

### BIRDS AND BEASTS
*Mythical and unlikely animals feature, along with the more mundane pigeon.*

*straw*

*burnt sienna*

### HERITAGE
*The shape, colours and decoration of this tine box point to a European tradition.*

### BORDERS
*Simple designs make effective use of S-strokes, C-strokes and commas.*

*olive*

*red oxide*

*Prussian blue*

*rust*

### FLOWERS
Tulips, carnations and fuschias are among the most painted floral subjects.

### FRAKTUR
Watercoloured certificates celebrated each special occasion in the lives of German immigrants.

rust    peach

dusty blue    straw

### STROKEWORK
Dots and hatching are liberally used in American decorative painting.

yellow oxide    tomato

olive

### PATRIOTISM
George and Martha Washington become folk heroes on a bride box.

### HEARTS
This simple motif is popular in American decorative painting.

### HEX SIGNS
Designs such as these adorn many barns and dower chests in Pennsylvania.

pimento    yellow oxide

# PROJECT: DOWER CHEST

This project was designed from a dower chest dated 1804
which featured urns of stylized flowers on white panels.
These panels have been cleverly antiqued to give them
depth and dimension.

*Level of difficulty: Intermediate*

Basecoater

Ruler

Masking
tape

## PROJECT OVERVIEW

- SURFACE PREPARATION *(see page 137)*
- UNDERCOATING *(see below)*
- ADDING PANELS AND GOLD *(see below)*
- BASECOATING *(see page 141)*
- TRANSFERRING DESIGN *(see page 136)*
- DISTRESSING GOLD *(see below)*
- PAINTING DESIGN *(see below)*
- DISTRESSING *(see page 142)*
- ANTIQUING *(see page 143)*
- VARNISHING *(see page 143)*
- GOLD WAXING *(see page 143)*
- WAXING *(see page 143)*

#8 flat

Chalk pencil

Spatula

Tracing &
transfer paper

Gold wax

Wax

Varnish

Wet-&-dry

Paint
palette

Razor

Kneaded
eraser

Stylus

#3 flat

#3 round

#1 liner

#8 bristle

Patina

Oil paint,
cloth & tissue

## PAINTING STEP-BY-STEP

**1** Prepare the surface. Undercoat in rust. Transfer two panels with a chalk pencil and ruler. Using a #8 flat, paint patches of gold scattered over the chest, including several within each panel.

**2** Make a rough sketch of the two panels on paper, noting the position of the gold patches. Use a #8 flat brush to paint three coats of white within each of the panels.

**3** Using a basecoating brush, paint two coats of dusty blue all over the chest, excluding the panels. Transfer the design (page 162) onto each of the panels.

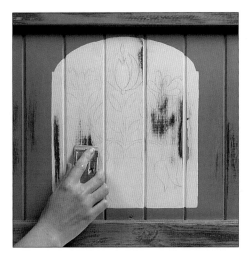

**4** Referring to your sketch, heavily distress the gold areas of the panels with a razor, scraping right back to expose some of the woodgrain.

**5** See overleaf for painting stages. Paint the leaves and flowers with a #3 round using the wet-on-wet technique. Block in the vase with a #3 flat brush and scratch lines with a stylus.

**6** When dry, erase all lines. Lightly distress the design with wet-and-dry paper. Antique and varnish. Using a cloth, apply gold wax around the rim and edges. Polish with clear wax to complete.

## DOUBLE-LOADING

Double-loading produces a stroke with two colours which merge but remain distinct. It can be very effective on leaves and petals which are painted with comma strokes, giving them a softly shaded quality. A combination of a light and dark colour works best.

**1** Wipe the brush through the main colour, turning and wiping again so that it is thoroughly loaded with paint.

**2** Take a single wipe through the edge of the contrasting colour.

**3** Use the double-loaded brush to paint blended strokes, reloading the brush as required.

## TULIP PAINTING STAGES

*Paint central petals with
double-loaded brush.*

pale orange      orange

rust      white

*Paint outer petals and add overstrokes.*

rust    yellow oxide    Prussian blue

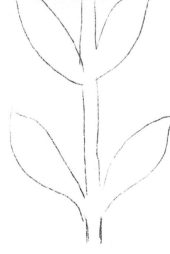

*Complete petals and paint leaves and stem
with double-loaded brush.*

dusty blue    Prussian blue    spruce    yellow oxide    white

# PROJECT: AMERICAN TOLEWARE

Painting on tinware developed in the New England states where utensils such as this document tin and coffee pot were basecoated in black or asphaltum and then decorated. In Pennsylvania, a red background and brighter designs were more common.

*Level of difficulty: Intermediate*

Basecoater

Ruler

Masking
tape

PROJECT OVERVIEW

- SURFACE PREPARATION (see page 137)
- BASECOATING (see page 141)
- ADDING BORDER (see below)
- TRANSFERRING DESIGN (see page 136)
- PAINTING DESIGN (see below)
- ANTIQUING (see page 143)
- VARNISHING (see page 143)

Kneaded
eraser

Varnish

Chalk pencil

Tracing &
transfer paper

Spatula

Stylus

#3 flat

#3 round

#1 liner

Paint
palette

Patina

Oil paint,
cloth &
tissue for
antiquing

#8 bristle

## PAINTING STEP-BY-STEP

**1** Prepare the surface. Basecoat with black. Using a chalk pencil and ruler, mark the border where appropriate. Paint three coats of cream on the border, using a #3 flat brush.

**2** Transfer the designs (pages 163-4) onto the front and sides of the box, using light transfer paper for the main design and dark transfer paper for the border design.

**3** See overleaf for painting stages. Paint the leaves and flowers wet-on-wet with a #3 round brush. Leave to dry. Add detail with a #1 liner. Paint ivory dots with the end of a brush.

**4** Paint the border design in red oxide with a fine point #3 round brush. When dry, erase all design lines.

**5** On the top of the box (or wherever appropriate) add gold trim lines. Paint the thin line with a #1 liner and thicker lines with a #3 round brush.

**6** Paint a gold flourish with a #3 round brush. Leave to dry. Antique and varnish to complete.

## FLOWER PAINTING STAGES

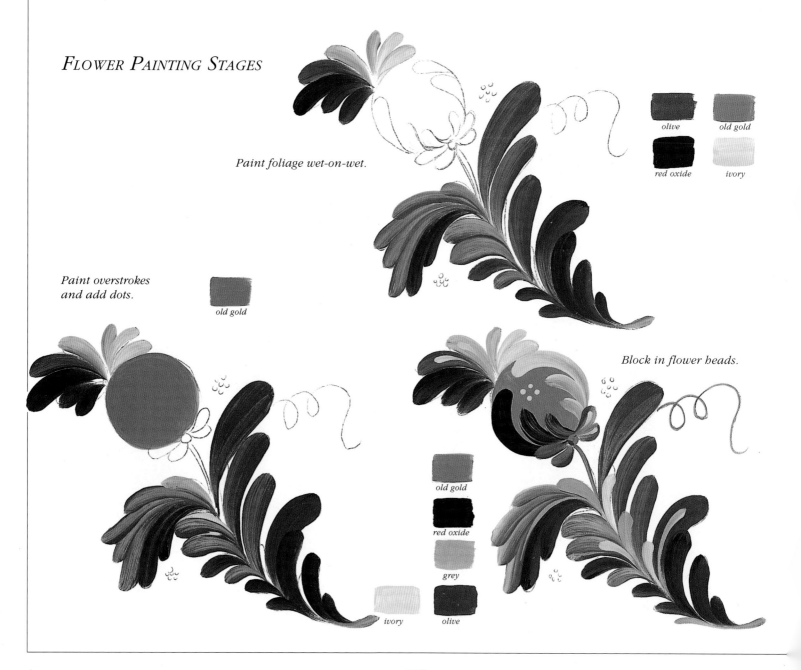

*Paint foliage wet-on-wet.*

olive

old gold

red oxide

ivory

*Paint overstrokes and add dots.*

old gold

*Block in flower heads.*

old gold

red oxide

grey

ivory

olive

## COFFEE POT PAINTING STAGES

*Paint foliage wet-on-wet.*

*olive*

*old gold*

*red oxide*

*ivory*

*Block in flower heads.*

*old gold*

*red oxide*

*ivory*

*Paint overstrokes
and add dots.*

*old gold*

*red oxide*

*olive*

*ivory*

*grey*

# MEDITERRANEAN STYLE

*The civilizations of the Mediterranean have always been influential in design: the ancient Greeks and Romans provided the very basis of Western decoration. Although the Italians flirted with the extremes of Baroque and Rococo, the hallmarks of Mediterranean style today are simple motifs and pure colours.*

*Italian clock*

Decorative painting in this part of the world is associated with ceramics rather than with wood. The Greeks often painted pottery vessels for holding wine or oil, leaving the red clay to show through the black design. As well as the human figure, these vases bore geometric borders, stylized acanthus leaves, bunches of grapes and other fruit. These motifs would reappear centuries later in the vocabulary of the neo-classical style.

The Moorish occupation of southern Spain lasted for centuries and left a strong Islamic mark, even after Christians reclaimed the area. Brilliantly coloured mosaics, intricate plasterwork and gilded sunbursts still adorn the buildings of Andalusia.

Europe's love of painted furniture in the eighteenth century had little affect on such remote areas of the Mediterranean. The greatest impact was in the north of Italy where the country people had contact with their Swiss and Austrian counterparts. Bedheads, armoires, chests and other provincial pieces were painted in Tuscany, Lombardy and the Veneto during this period and the floral designs reveal the northern influence.

In present times, Mediterranean decoration is most common on ceramics. Markets in Greece, Spain and Italy overflow with brightly painted tiles, plates and pots. In these countries, tiles are not

*Ceramic plate*

simply used as a floor covering: they might adorn plain chests or feature on window boxes. Tiles often cover inside and outside walls, sometimes serving as a canvas for a large-scale picture instead of a series of repeated designs. There are some regional differences in ceramic painting: vivid yellow and green are favoured in Spain and Portugal, while blue and white are popular in Italy and Greece. The motifs vary slightly but, in general, there is no mistaking the bold lines and confident colours of Mediterranean design.

*Blue and white— the colours that summon Mediterranean style to mind—add charm to a Spanish street.*

*Ceramic tiles form a religious tableau.*

# DESIGNS AND VARIATIONS

Most painting in Greece, Italy and Spain is executed on ceramics. So, a simple step towards recreating the Mediterranean style is to paint on a white background. Designs are worked in pure colours and shading is achieved by floating one colour rather than blending. The result has a fresh and clean feel which has great appeal for those of us surrounded by cluttered modern images.

**FOLIAGE**
*The classic acanthus leaf is used as a free-standing element.*

**FLORENTINE**
*These brooches draw on Italian decoration for inspiration.*

**FRUIT**
*The seasonal harvest makes colourful subject matter.*

olive

grape

mauve

rust

**PATTERNS**
*Daisies, anthemions and quatrefoils can be repeated to create decorative patterns.*

**EMBLEMS**
*A flower is treated in such a stylized way that it becomes pure ornament.*

peach    dusty blue

## BORDERS
*Stylized leaves and flowers are well-suited for strip patterns.*

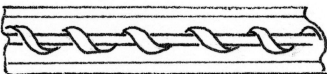

## BEASTS
*The cockerel is a traditional Spanish motif. Fish often feature in Italian design.*

dusty blue    Prussian blue

## TREE OF LIFE
*A Mediterranean version of the emblem is shown on this Italian dish.*

## FLORALS
*Flowers are represented simply, and are generally shown front on.*

yellow    Prussian blue

charcoal

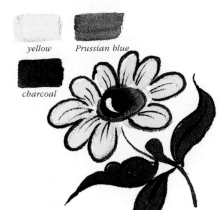

107

# PROJECT: ITALIAN PLATTER

The fresh white background and clean blue lines of this simple
design sum up Mediterranean style. We have chosen a wooden
platter sealed with gesso; you may prefer to work with ceramics
paints to decorate a ceramic plate or series of tiles.

*Level of difficulty: Beginner*

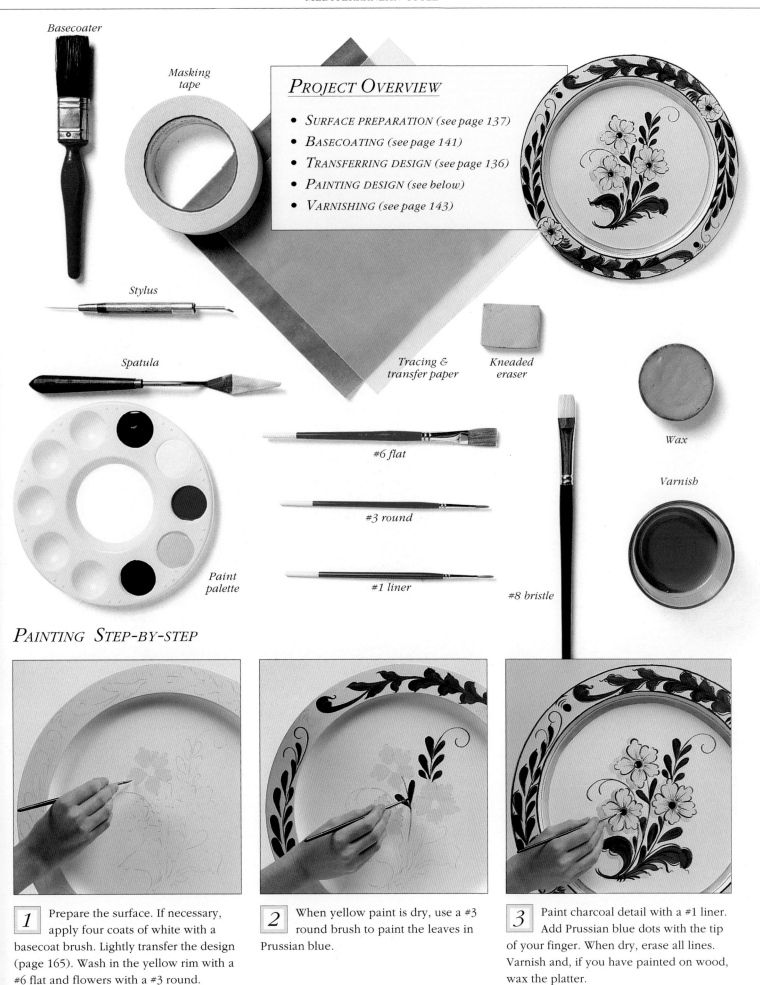

Basecoater

Masking tape

PROJECT OVERVIEW

• SURFACE PREPARATION (see page 137)
• BASECOATING (see page 141)
• TRANSFERRING DESIGN (see page 136)
• PAINTING DESIGN (see below)
• VARNISHING (see page 143)

Stylus

Spatula

Tracing & transfer paper

Kneaded eraser

Wax

#6 flat

Varnish

#3 round

Paint palette

#1 liner

#8 bristle

## PAINTING STEP-BY-STEP

1  Prepare the surface. If necessary, apply four coats of white with a basecoat brush. Lightly transfer the design (page 165). Wash in the yellow rim with a #6 flat and flowers with a #3 round.

2  When yellow paint is dry, use a #3 round brush to paint the leaves in Prussian blue.

3  Paint charcoal detail with a #1 liner. Add Prussian blue dots with the tip of your finger. When dry, erase all lines. Varnish and, if you have painted on wood, wax the platter.

# EASTERN SLAVIC FOLK ART

*THE SLAVIC PEOPLES OF RUSSIA, Byelorussia and Ukraine each have their own culture, language and history, but they share a love of colourful decoration. Some elements of painting—the distinctive use of red, for example—are common throughout these countries. Other traditions are distinctively regional.*

*Khokhloma ware*

Painting is one of the richest branches of Slavic folk art and has its beginnings in Ukrainian wall paintings, created with a feather, reeds, or straw wisps. Flowers, pine boughs, oak leaves, birds and animals all decorated walls above the hearth and bed, or the ceiling and beams. The colours, originally made from plants, were applied on a white, blue or green background and had to be repainted regularly. In the sixteenth century, however, people turned to painting on sheets of paper. These *malyovki* were painted when farm work permitted, generally in winter, and were glued on the walls for important festivities. Domestic articles were also painted, including wooden bread plates, sleds, distaffs for spinning flax, and *skrinyas* or chests for storing holiday clothing.

The village of Petrikivka in eastern Ukraine is famous for its floral painting. Most designs follow the tradition of painting three main flowers, symbolic of the Holy Trinity. Petrikivka

*Soldiers, like children, are attracted by the bright Slavic paintwork of a Russian fairground.*

*Russian pokerwork*

artists use brushes made of cats' hair, capable of both heavy strokes and extremely fine hatch lines, and they add egg to paint to intensify the colour and make brushstrokes more expressive. They also employ a series of brushstrokes which makes their work quite distinct.

The Volga region of Russia, on the other hand, is renowned for its dramatic lacquerware. Craftsmen in Khokhloma had long been making wooden utensils and painting them with exuberant red and black leaf designs and a protective coat of varnish. They knew that varnish turns yellow when heated and found that yellowed varnish over tin produces a rich gold finish. They adapted this to suit the wooden spoons and bowls made locally, soaking them in linseed oil and then rubbing with powdered tin, painting, lacquering and finally firing them. Today this peasants' gold, decorated with swirling motifs, can be achieved with modern acrylics.

*Ukrainian plate*

While design and style vary across regions and countries, the folk painting of Eastern Slavic nations is generally vibrant in colour and rich in symbolism.

# DESIGNS AND VARIATIONS

For the Eastern Slavs, colours have symbolic meaning and carry clear messages for the viewer. White represents purity and innocence, yellow speaks of the harvest and hospitality, while the blue of the sky is the colour of good health. Red, the most commonly painted colour throughout the region, signifies happiness, hope and passion.

tomato

rust    olive

## PETRIKIVKA
*Stylized flowers in bright colours are the speciality of this Ukrainian town.*

## BORDERS
*Choose from floral shapes or simple geometrics in contrasting colours.*

black

Prussian blue

red

## BIRDS
*For Ukrainians, a perched bird represents a protector of hearth and home.*

## ROSETTES
*These circular patterns derive from the Slavic symbol for the pagan sun-god.*

yellow oxide    orange

burnt sienna

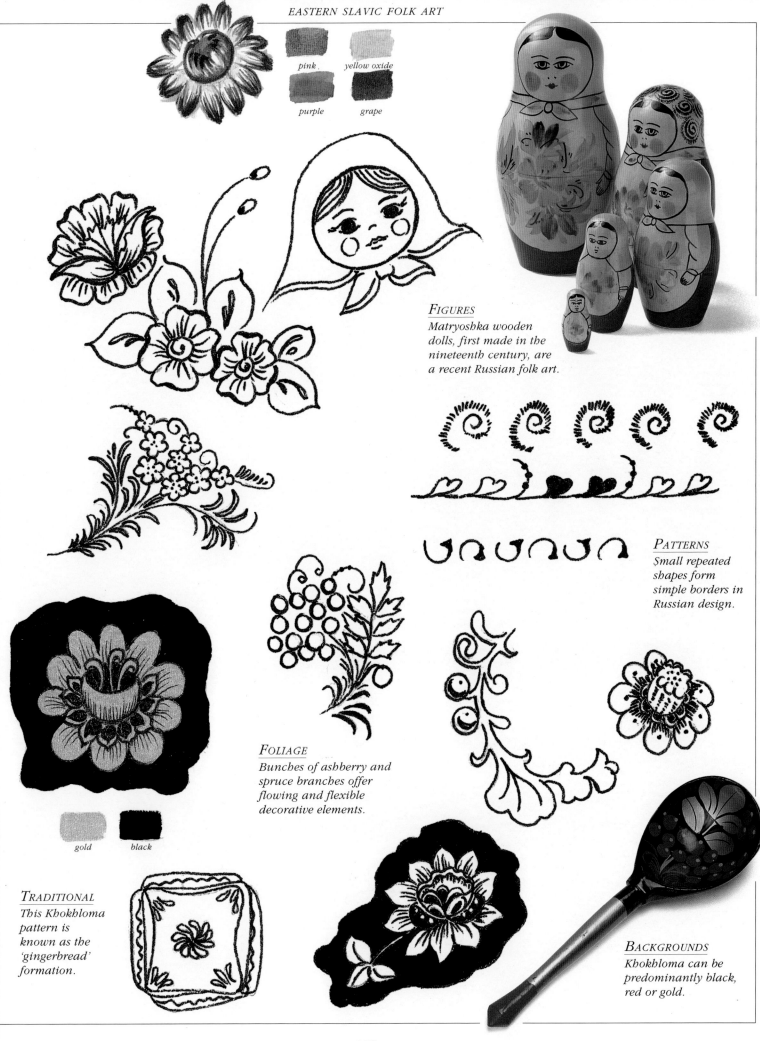

pink

yellow oxide

purple

grape

**FIGURES**
Matryoshka wooden
dolls, first made in the
nineteenth century, are
a recent Russian folk art.

**PATTERNS**
Small repeated
shapes form
simple borders in
Russian design.

**FOLIAGE**
Bunches of ashberry and
spruce branches offer
flowing and flexible
decorative elements.

gold

black

**TRADITIONAL**
This Khokhloma
pattern is
known as the
'gingerbread'
formation.

**BACKGROUNDS**
Khokhloma can be
predominantly black,
red or gold.

# PROJECT: SLAVIC EGGS

The tradition of painting Easter eggs, known as *psyanka* in Ukraine, offers endless opportunities for decorative painters. The large wooden eggs shown below have been painted with a Russian matryoshka design and two Ukrainian geometric patterns.

*Level of difficulty: Beginner*

#6 flat    Pencil

## PROJECT OVERVIEW

- SURFACE PREPARATION (*see page 137*)
- BASECOATING (*see page 141*)
- TRANSFERRING DESIGN (*see page 136*)
- PAINTING DESIGN (*see below*)
- ANTIQUING (*see page 143*)
- VARNISHING (*see page 143*)
- WAXING (*see page 143*)

Kneaded eraser

Spatula

#3 flat

#3 round

#1 liner

#8 bristle

Paint palette

Varnish

Wax

Patina

Oil paint, cloth & tissue for antiquing

## PAINTING STEP-BY-STEP

**1** Prepare the surface, emptying a fresh egg or sealing a wooden one. Basecoat white with a #6 flat. Draw the design (page 168) freehand in pencil, omitting detail.

**2** Using a #3 flat brush, paint the black dress and yellow shawl. Paint a second coat over each colour.

**3** Freehand, paint the flowers and foliage white with a #3 round brush. Use the design for reference.

**4** Paint the flesh in apricot, using a #3 flat brush for the face and a #3 round brush for the hands. Repeat with a second coat.

**5** Wash in the pink and purple flowers with a #3 round and a #1 liner. Paint hair burnt sienna and add lips and cheeks.

**6** Paint black eyes, nose and details with a #1 liner. When dry, antique lightly, then varnish and wax to complete.

## ORNATE EGG PAINTING STAGES

*Add overstrokes and detail.*

*Wash in base design colours.*

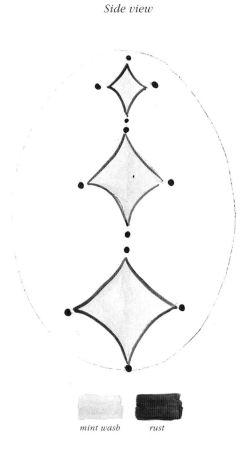

*Side view*

*rust*      *black*

*mint wash*      *rust wash*      *yellow wash*

*mint wash*      *rust*

# HATCHED EGG PAINTING STAGES

*Basecoat quadrants
and circular patches.*

*Complete flower, ribbon trims
and white detail.*

*Add hatching, ribbon
marks and petals.*

black   rust

sunflower   white

rust   black

rust   black   white

# PROJECT: KHOKHLOMA TRAY

Gold, fiery red and black—the rich colours of Russian khokhloma—
produce an extremely dramatic effect. The project is easier than it
appears; however, the careful layering of colours and final
varnishing will take some time and a degree of patience.

*Level of difficulty: Intermediate*

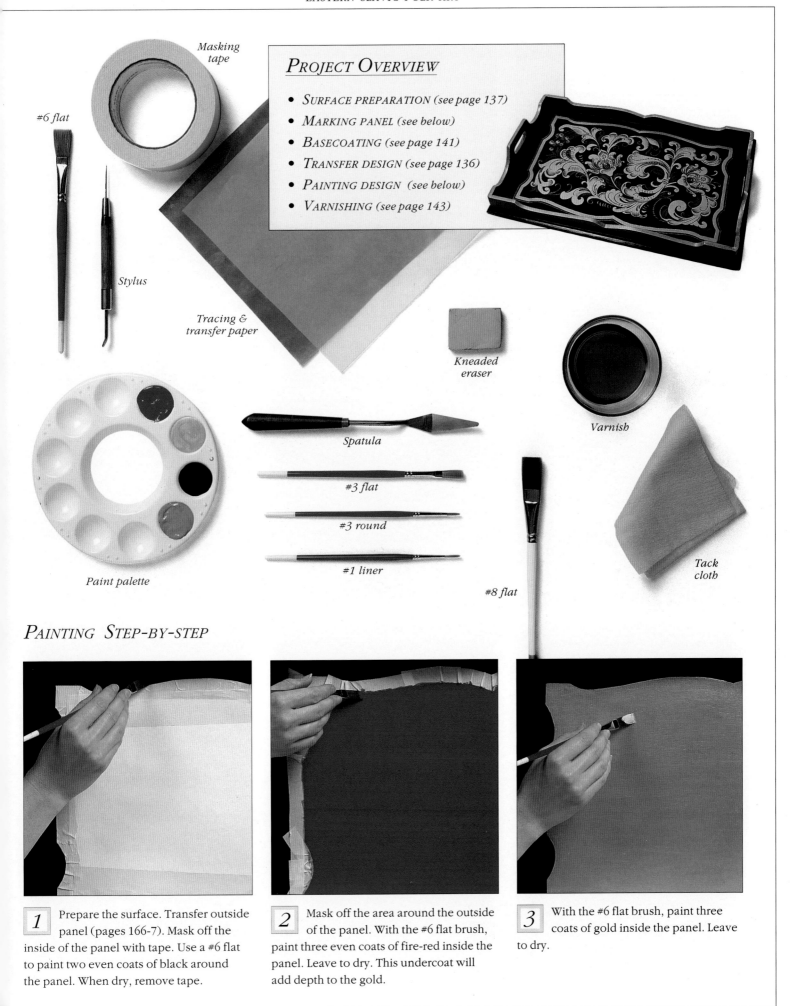

*Masking tape*

*#6 flat*

*Stylus*

## PROJECT OVERVIEW

- SURFACE PREPARATION (see page 137)
- MARKING PANEL (see below)
- BASECOATING (see page 141)
- TRANSFER DESIGN (see page 136)
- PAINTING DESIGN (see below)
- VARNISHING (see page 143)

*Tracing & transfer paper*

*Kneaded eraser*

*Varnish*

*Paint palette*

*Spatula*

*#3 flat*

*#3 round*

*#1 liner*

*#8 flat*

*Tack cloth*

## PAINTING STEP-BY-STEP

**1** Prepare the surface. Transfer outside panel (pages 166-7). Mask off the inside of the panel with tape. Use a #6 flat to paint two even coats of black around the panel. When dry, remove tape.

**2** Mask off the area around the outside of the panel. With the #6 flat brush, paint three even coats of fire-red inside the panel. Leave to dry. This undercoat will add depth to the gold.

**3** With the #6 flat brush, paint three coats of gold inside the panel. Leave to dry.

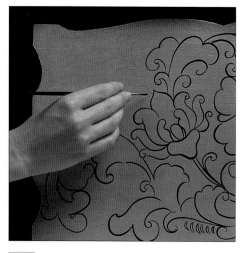

**4** Remove the masking tape. Using dark transfer paper and a stylus, transfer the design (page 166-7).

**5** Carefully paint the black outlining with a #1 liner. Leave to dry.

**6** Block in black areas with a #3 flat brush, leaving a gold trim line around the panel. Strengthen black areas with a second coat.

**7** Add black detail with a #1 liner and the black dots with the end of a stylus or brush. Block in the orange-red with a #3 round brush.

**8** Paint gold overstrokes with a #1 liner. Add a gold border with a #3 flat brush and strengthen the gold trim with the #1 liner.

**9** When dry, wipe with a tack cloth to remove dust. Using a #8 flat, apply ten coats of gloss varnish, sanding between coats and drying in a dust-free place.

## BERRIES PAINTING STAGES

*Basecoat in gold and transfer design.*    *Outline in black.*    *Block in fire red and add black detail.*

# FLOWER PAINTING STAGES

*Basecoat in gold
and transfer design.*

gold

*Outline in black.*

black

*Add black and fire red detail.*

black    fire red

# DECORATIVE PAINTING OF THE EAST

*IN STYLE AND CONTENT, Eastern decorative painting spans a wide range, from the subtle and harmonious approach of traditional Chinese watercolour painting to the more vivid and vigorous representations found in Japanese, Indonesian and Indian art. Each form offers much inspiration for the folk artist.*

*Japanese cabinet*

Of these countries, China has the longest history of painting, spanning over two thousand years. As the most advanced culture in Asia for centuries, the influence of Chinese art on its neighbours—Japan, Korea and Thailand—is still evident today. Other countries further west, such as Indonesia and India, came under the influence of Islamic cultures, revealed in their use of contrasting colours and repeated shapes.

The role of the artist in China and Japan was also greatly affected by religion. Many objects were painted for festivals, funerals and other rituals and though often destroyed during the ceremony, great care was taken with the decoration. The process of painting was valued as a spiritual activity and as an integral part of the ceremony itself. Religious belief also affected the subject matter. Taoists believe that all of life can be depicted in the smallest thing—a twig or a butterfly—hence the attention to detail in much Chinese painting.

Chinese artists mainly used watercolours and ink made from pine soot, so their work is characterized by a fluid brush-stroke which suggests forms rather than drawing them with precision. Ideograms, a form of Chinese script, were often included, expressing a line of poetry or a philosophical thought. Japanese painting also combines text and images in this way.

*18th century Chinese dish*

Throughout Asia, fans, umbrellas, boxes, bowls, trays and screens were commonly decorated items. In Japan and China, such wooden pieces were coated with a lacquer for strength and protection. Other Eastern artworks are less permanent: women in villages throughout India redecorate the entrance to their homes each day using pigments and coloured dust.

*An unusually bright rock painting in China reveals an Indian influence, carried through religion.*

*Masks for sale in a Singapore market*

# DESIGNS AND VARIATIONS

The Chinese were particularly skilled in the use of porcelain glazes; from a single red-oxide tint they could produce reds, browns, soft greens, blues and black, simply by varying the temperature of the kiln. These colours feature often in Eastern art, especially the combination of blue and white.

### ANIMALS
Cicadas, horses and other beasts feature along with the mythical lion-dog and dragon.

*dusty blue*   *Prussian blue*

### EMBLEMS
These heraldic devices are drawn from Japanese robes.

*rust*

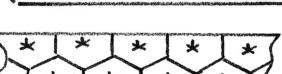

### BORDERS
Geometrics and flower shapes are simple basic units which can be combined in various borders.

### BIRDS
Swallows, cranes and the rising phoenix are popular Eastern motifs.

*dusty blue*   *Prussian blue*

**BAMBOO**
*Foliage such as bamboo or reeds can be suggested with a few strokes.*

**SEASONS**
*Prunus, peony, chrysanthemum and lotus are used to represent the seasonal cycle.*

**COLOURS**
*Red and gold, which represent prosperity and good fortune, are combined with black in the project overleaf.*

gold

xmas red    black

gold

black

Prussian blue

**PATTERNS**
*Stylized flowers are the blocks for building effective patterns.*

**SYMBOLS**
*Buddhist symbols include the Wheel of the Law and the mystic knot.*

# PROJECT: EASTERN LACQUERWARE

True Japanese lacquer is made from a tree sap and is a rare commodity. Various finishes have been developed to emulate its sheen; this one is known as *negoro nuri*. The design features cherry blossom, a favourite subject of both Chinese and Japanese decorative artists.

*Level of difficulty: Intermediate*

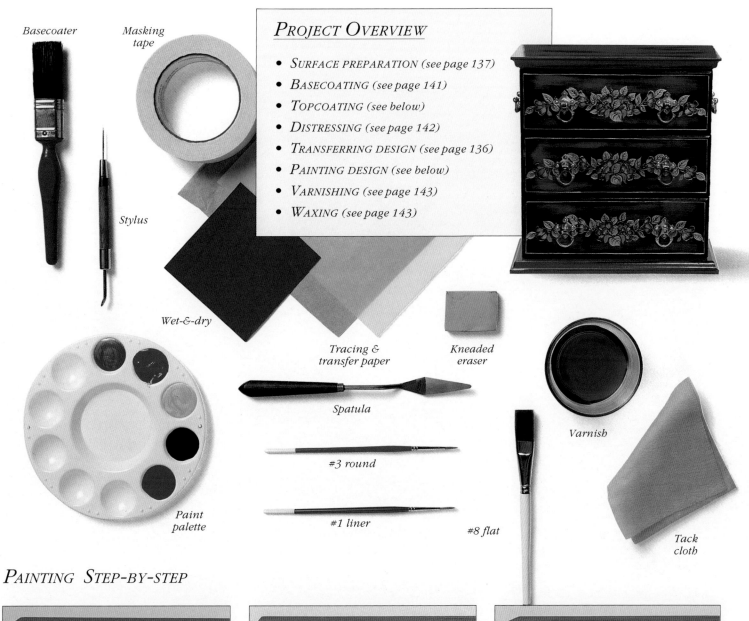

Basecoater

Masking tape

Stylus

Wet-&-dry

### PROJECT OVERVIEW

- SURFACE PREPARATION (see page 137)
- BASECOATING (see page 141)
- TOPCOATING (see below)
- DISTRESSING (see page 142)
- TRANSFERRING DESIGN (see page 136)
- PAINTING DESIGN (see below)
- VARNISHING (see page 143)
- WAXING (see page 143)

Tracing & transfer paper

Kneaded eraser

Spatula

#3 round

#1 liner

#8 flat

Paint palette

Varnish

Tack cloth

## PAINTING STEP-BY-STEP

**1** Prepare the surface. Basecoat drawers with three coats of xmas red and the remainder of the chest with three coats of black. Topcoat each drawer in black and the remainder in xmas red. Distress with wet-and-dry paper.

**2** Using light transfer paper and a stylus, transfer the design (page 169). Using a #3 round brush, block in some leaves and petals with gold and others in copper. Paint gold detail and trim line with a #1 liner. Leave to dry.

**3** Add black detail with a #1 liner. When dry, erase lines and wipe with a tack cloth to remove dust. Using a #8 flat brush, apply ten coats of gloss varnish, sanding between coats and drying in a dust-free environment.

# ENGLISH ROSES
# AND CASTLES

*THE FOLK ART of most countries is an established tradition with a long history. By comparison, the romantically named Roses and Castles is a young style of painting, having developed within the last two hundred years as a striking way of decorating English narrow boats.*

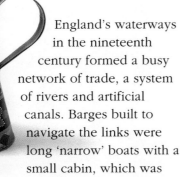

*Tin tankard*

England's waterways in the nineteenth century formed a busy network of trade, a system of rivers and artificial canals. Barges built to navigate the links were long 'narrow' boats with a small cabin, which was home to the boatman and often to a crew of wife and family. The canal folk formed a community and, to emphasize their difference from the rest of society, they wore an outdated style of costume and decorated their boat-homes with painted designs.

These designs included generous swags of roses and romantic land-scapes complete with turrets, hence the name 'Roses and Castles'. As well, geometric patterns and motifs from playing cards featured on hatches and panels. Implements such as navigation lamps, coal boxes and tinware utensils were all brightly painted.

For such a recent folk art, the origins of the Roses and Castles style are well hidden. The strong colours and rich patterns suggest a connection with Romany gypsies, but paintwork on gypsy wagons is more Baroque in character. Dutch folk artists painted flowers shaped like those on English narrow boats, yet there the similarity ends. Most likely, the canal painters were influenced by commercial painters in the Birmingham area, the centre of the canal system, where japanned tinware was decorated with floral designs and landscapes for the masses.

*Table-cupboard*

The painting process had to combine speed and durability. Each panel was primed and painted with two coats of flat paint. The design was painted on top of this with quick, confident brush-strokes and, when completely dry, it was varnished for protection. Brightness was important; panels were not allowed to age, but were painted afresh to convey the boatmen and women's pride in their unusual way of life.

*This narrow boat is decked with both real and painted flowers; it also bears a colourful diamond pattern along its side.*

*Two regional styles of paintwork: the cabin block and small cans are painted with free-flowing brushstrokes; the handbowl bears realistic cabbage roses.*

# DESIGNS AND VARIATIONS

Roses and Castles is not a subtle style: its bright colours and strong lines are designed to catch the eye. Following tradition, the decorative elements are painted quickly because the cost and speed of boat painting was a concern for canal folk. Stylized flowers and idealized landscapes are combined with geometric motifs to create a lively form of decoration.

## FLOWERS & LEAVES
*Roses are painted in quick simple brush-strokes and the basic leaf shape is varied by highlighting.*

## BORDERS
*Crescent shapes and multicoloured diamonds offer simple but effective borders.*

## HATCH DESIGNS
*Playing-card symbols, often painted on cabin hatches, can be used to fill small panels.*

## GARLANDS
*Strings of daisies, another featured flower, alternate with bands of roses on this water jug.*

*xmas red*    *yellow oxide*    *French blue*

*black*    *xmas red*    *yellow oxide*

**PATTERNS**
Garlands of flowers can be arranged to suit the shape and space available.

red oxide

xmas red

white

orange

sunflower

white

rose pink

xmas red

white

white

**CASTLES**
Scenes are often naive, as on this cabin block.

**BACKGROUNDS**
Dark colours are used for basecoats and should be painted evenly on the surface.

black

forest green

xmas red

# PROJECT: MILK CHURN

Water cans were commonly decorated utensils on narrow boats.
In this advanced project, a milk churn is adorned with a garlanded
scene and a swag of roses; these elements could also be used
separately on smaller items.

*Level of difficulty: Advanced*

Basecoater    #8 flat    Masking tape

## PROJECT OVERVIEW

- SURFACE PREPARATION (see page 137)
- BASECOATING (see page 141)
- ADDING PANEL (see below)
- TRANSFERRING DESIGN (see page 136)
- PAINTING DESIGN (see below)
- ANTIQUING (see page 143)
- VARNISHING (see page 143)

Stylus

Tracing & transfer paper

Spatula

Kneaded eraser

#8 bristle

Varnish

#6 flat

#3 flat

#3 round

Worn brush

Paint palette

#1 liner

Patina

Oil paint, cloth & tissue for antiquing

## PAINTING STEP-BY-STEP

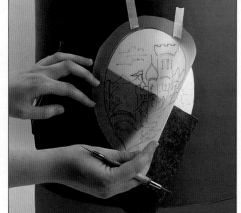

**1** Prepare the surface and undercoat bands white. Basecoat churn in forest green with xmas red bands. Transfer the oval outline only (page 170) and, using a #8 flat, paint oval with three coats of white. When dry, transfer castle design.

**2** See overleaf for painting stages. Block in sky with a #6 flat. Paint clouds with a sideloaded #3 flat. Wash in foreground and block in buildings with a #3 flat. Use a worn brush to paint bushes. Detail with a #1 liner.

**3** When castle scene is dry, transfer the surrounding garland design (page 170). Block in leaves and flowers with a #3 round brush. See overleaf for swag painting stages.

4 Use a #3 round brush to paint overstrokes on the roses and daisies. Refer below for colours and brushstrokes when painting the flowers and leaves.

5 Use a #3 round brush to paint overstrokes on leaves. Complete the garland surrounding the castle scene and the swag of flowers on the top of the churn.

6 Use a #1 liner to paint fine yellow lines on the red bands. Leave to dry. Erase all lines, then antique the churn and varnish to complete.

## SWAG PAINTING STAGES

*Block in leaves.*

olive

pimento

*Block in petals.*

pimento

yellow oxide

rose pink

burnt umber

French blue

*Paint overstrokes.*

xmas red

sunflower

white

## CASTLE PAINTING STAGES

*Wash in sky and water.*

*Block in buildings
and background.*

*dusty blue wash*

*Prussian blue wash*

*apricot*

*Wash in foreground.*

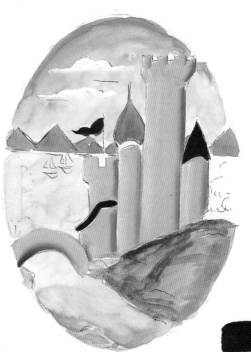

*tomato*

*spruce wash*     *olive wash*

*Complete bushes
and add detail.*

*black*

*white*

# GENERAL INFORMATION

*The emphasis of this book is design, rather than technique, which is why this chapter appears at the back and not as the introduction. The information that follows offers a grounding in the basic methods of decorative painting but is not intended as a set of rules. In decorative painting, there are no real rules and each person develops an individual approach to the craft.*

## DESIGN AND SCALING

The articles painted in the projects are suggestions only; it may not be possible to locate a similar piece or it may not suit your home. Choose items that are in keeping with the style in which you wish to paint. Likewise, you may wish to vary the colour scheme or modify a motif or border. If so, you will find the Designs and Variations pages a good reference point.

*A small design from the Moroccan shoe-box has been scaled up in size.*

Many projects have several designs for different sides; you might find that not all are necessary.

Having chosen an article, decide whether the design will need to be adapted to fit a panel by repeating an element or deleting a section. If the basic proportions are suitable, assess whether the design needs to be enlarged or reduced.

To enlarge or reduce a design, first transfer it onto tracing paper and draw a grid over it, numbering each square. Take another piece of tracing paper the size of the panel or area to be painted, and draw a grid with the same amount of squares, numbering each square to correspond with those on the original tracing. On the second grid, copy the detail from the original grid square by square. An even easier method is to use a photocopying machine to enlarge or reduce your design by the required percentage.

To transfer the design onto a panel, place tracing paper over the design and trace the lines using a pen or pencil. Position the tracing on the painting surface and hold it in place with masking tape. Insert a sheet of transfer paper between the tracing and painting surface so that the coated side is facing the latter. Run the end of a stylus over the design using light pressure. Draw in the main lines only, leaving any finer detail that would be covered by base strokes.

For some symmetrical designs, only half the design is given in the back of the book. Where a dashed line appears, trace the half supplied then flip your tracing to complete the design. There are also some repeat designs of which only a sample section has been supplied. An arrow beside a design indicates that it should be turned so the arrow points up.

# PREPARATION

While surface preparation is less interesting than painting the design, it is a necessary stage in a successful project. Most of the projects in this book have been painted on wood, however many other surfaces can be painted. Choose your surface keeping in mind the purpose to which the piece will be put. Carefully follow the preparation stages for the relevant surface.

## NEW WOOD

Fill any holes with a commercial wood filler. Always allow the filler to dry thoroughly. Sand lightly with a medium grade sandpaper and then seal with a sealer or water-based varnish. When the sealer is dry, sand lightly with fine sandpaper.

## OLD WOOD

If the finish on your old wooden article is good (not chipped, cracked, or peeling) then simply sand lightly and basecoat over the top. However, if the paint is cracked or peeling, it will need to be removed for a smooth surface. Old paint and varnish can be softened with a commercial paint stripper and then removed with a paint scraper. Smooth with a course sandpaper or some steel wool. Seal the article as for new wood.

If the old finish is good but dark and you plan to paint a light coloured background, sand lightly and then paint the whole article with gesso. When dry, sand lightly.

## NEW METAL

Scrub the article in soapy water using steel wool. Rinse in equal parts of water and vinegar. Dry the article thoroughly. Spray or paint on a rust-inhibiting primer. Leave to dry for at least twenty-four hours.

## OLD METAL

If the article is painted, first strip with paint stripper. Remove any rust with a wire brush or steel wool. Badly rusted articles will require an application of a commercial rust converter. Clean, rinse and prime the article as for new metal.

*Some of the materials for such surface preparation techniques as sanding, sealing and undercoating.*

## PAPIER-MÂCHÉ

Whether you have moulded your own or purchased a commercial papier-mâché piece, it will need no surface preparation. The surface is smooth and is already sealed with the paper and glue.

## TERRACOTTA

Submerge the terracotta article in water. When the water has soaked in, remove the article and lay it upside down on a towel. Allow the article to half-dry and then paint the outside with sealer or water-based varnish. When this coat is completely dry, apply sealer to the inside of the article and leave to dry for a least twenty-four hours before painting.

# MATERIALS

## ACRYLIC PAINTS
All projects were painted with acrylics, which are quick drying and clean up with water. There are several commercial brands of acrylics designed for folk art and these offer a range of premixed colours.

## WAXES
Clear wax and gold wax are used to finish many projects.

## OIL PAINTS
A few toner colours are needed for antiquing.

## CONTAINERS
Film containers are useful for storing unused paint; a palette is essential for mixing paints.

## PICKLING SOLUTION
A mixture of white paint and sealer for whitewashing raw wood.

## PATINA
A mixture of turpentine and linseed oil for antiquing.

## CRACKLE MEDIUM
A product which makes paint crack; available as an undercoat or topcoat medium.

## SPATULA
A palette knife is useful for mixing colours.

## BRUSHES
A # symbol denotes brush size or number. A basic kit includes a basecoater, round and flat brushes and a liner. Old brushes are useful for special effects. To care for brushes, rinse in water, wash in soap and gently shape tip into a point. Store upright.

## VARNISH
Satin finish is generally recommended.

## CLOTHS
Openweave cloth, soft cotton rags and paper tissues are essential.

## GLOVES
Protect hands when antiquing.

## MASKING TAPE
Paper-backed tape for transferring designs and masking off sections.

**COTTON BUDS**
Moisten with methylated spirits and use for cleaning up errors.

**RAZOR**
For stripping or heavy distressing.

**ABRASIVES**
Use sandpaper and steel wool for preparation and finishing; use moistened wet-and-dry (or silicon carbide) to distress pieces.

**SCRAP PAPER**
You will need paper towels and newspaper.

**PATTERNING TOOLS**
Cardboard combs and plastic wrap are useful for dragging and smudging.

**PENCILS**
Use chalk pencil on dark surfaces and carbon on light colours.

**SEA SPONGE**
Applies paint or any other medium in a subtle manner.

**STYLUS**
To transfer designs and paint small dots.

**COMPASS**
Useful for marking borders.

**PASTE**
Use a kleister medium or cornflour paste for woodgraining.

**RETARDER**
A commercial medium, also known as extender, for lengthening the drying time of acrylic paint. Dip brushes in retarder before loading, or mix retarder into paint.

**MAULSTICK**
A padded length of wood for steadying the hand and keeping elbows off wet areas.

**THREAD**
Thick cotton thread is used for making drag marks.

**MEASURING TOOLS**
A ruler, set square and tape measure are useful for marking panels.

**KNEADED ERASER**
For removing design lines after painting.

**TOOTHBRUSH**
A old toothbrush is ideal for spattering.

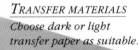

**TACK CLOTH**
Cheesecloth impregnated with linseed oil for removing dust; store in an airtight container.

**PIPING BAG**
Used for working a relief pattern on a surface.

**TRANSFER MATERIALS**
Choose dark or light transfer paper as suitable. Tracing paper is available in various thicknesses.

# PAINTING TECHNIQUES

This section provides information on the brushstrokes, backgrounds, imitation finishes and aging
techniques used in decorative painting.

## BRUSHSTROKES

### COMMAS

The basic stroke of folk
painting is the comma, a
downward stroke with a
blunt head and a tail.

### FLOURISH

Commas can be
combined in
various ways.

### 'S' STROKES

Load brush with paint
and roll tip to a point.
Lower and raise the
brush gently when
stroking to form a tail at
either end, with a twist
in the body.

### 'C' STROKES

Load brush with paint
and roll tip to a point.
Lower and raise the
brush gently when
stroking to form a tail
at either end, with a
curve in the body.

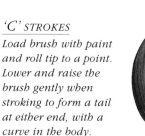

### TEARDROPS

Straight commas can
be used as central
petals or foliage.

### SHAPE FILLERS

To paint the daisy (left), block
in the base colours and
overstroke with commas and
teardrops; the tulip (right) is
a combination of 'C' strokes,
'S' strokes and commas.

### DOTS

Paint dots with the end of the brush or
a stylus, depending on the desired size.

### LINEWORK

Use a liner brush to paint detail and
trim lines. Paint should be a thin
consistency for free-flowing linework.

### SIDE-LOADING

Dress the brush
with one colour
and flatten to a
wedge. Side wipe
through a second,
contrasting colour.

### DOUBLE-LOADING

Dress the brush
lightly with the first
colour and then
sweep it through the
edge of the contrast
colour.

### FLOAT

Remove excess water from
brush, sideload with paint and
blend on the palette before
painting on the surface. Float
paint to form a ribbon (right).

## BLOCKING

Blocking is used to fill in an area with opaque paint.
A large flat brush is recommended to avoid uneven
brushstrokes. In the above example, the base colour
has been blocked in.

## WET-ON-WET

This technique shown above is used to achieve a soft blend
of colours and should be worked a small section at a time.
You can use retarder to extend painting time. Paint base
colour and, before it dries, apply the overstrokes.

## BASECOATING

Use a large, inexpensive brush and apply a smooth opaque coat of paint. Apply as many coats as necessary to cover the article adequately. Lightly sand in between coats.

## WASHING

Mix a thin colour wash by adding lots of water to your colour, creating a transparent glaze. Moisten the surface to be painted with a damp cloth. Use a large art brush for washing background areas and a #3 flat brush or smaller for washing within a design. Load the brush with paint and then touch the tip lightly on a paper towel to remove excess moisture. Paint a small section at a time, blending harsh edges. This sun design has been washed and partially floated.

## SPONGING

Submerge a natural sea sponge in water and then wring it out. Lightly load the sponge with paint and dab the excess on a piece of waste paper. Hold the sponge lightly and pat the paint on to the article, gradually building up to the required colour density. For further illustration, see page 23.

## SCRATCHING

Lightly seal the area with sealer or water-based varnish. Topcoat with paint and while the paint is still wet, use a stylus or the blunt end of a paint brush to scratch away a design.

## PICKLING

Pickling is a pale whitewashed effect for raw wood. A commercial pickling medium can be used or you can make your own by diluting white paint with sealer or water-based varnish. Dampen the wood with a cloth. Apply the pickling solution with a large flat brush, painting with the grain of the wood. Wipe off the excess with a soft clean cloth. Repeat this process to intensify the colour.

## GLAZING

Rather than basecoat over wood with an attractive grain, consider glazing or staining it. Use a commercial stain or mix five parts sealer (or water-based varnish) with one part paint. Suitable colours are raw sienna, brown earth and burnt sienna. Apply with a large flat brush or soft cloth in the direction of the grain. Use long smooth strokes and wipe off the excess with a spare soft cloth. Work quickly, glazing a small area at a time.

## RELIEF WORK

Use a cake decorator piping set with a fine nozzle filled with a thick bodied paint. Carefully pipe over the design. If the surface is curved, apply small sections at a time to avoid the paint running. Allow to dry for one to two days.

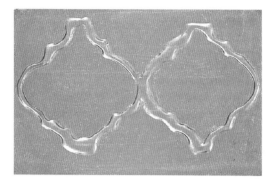

## DISTRESSING

To distress an article lightly, use wet-and-dry paper and detergent. Gently rub the painted surface along the grain of the wood. Continue rubbing until some of the basecoat colour has been revealed. For heavy distressing, use a scrapper or razor blade.

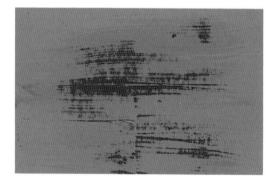

## MARBLING

Marble comes in many colours and forms and, accordingly, there are different marbling methods. The following method is perhaps the simplest. Paint retarder on to the basecoated surface to slow down the drying process and work a section at a time. Paint random lines in a contrasting colour with a #3 round brush, then smudge lines with a sponge or piece of crumpled plastic wrap, changing the angle so that the smudge mark changes also. Use a #1 liner or a feather to add fine veins of paint. For an example, see page 91.

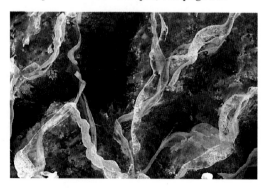

## DRY BRUSHING

Dress a large dry brush with paint, then wipe it on a paper towel to remove most of the colour. Paint on the desired area with short strokes in a dusting motion. Colour can be built up using continuous strokes.

## CRACKLING

Crackle medium separates the top layer of colour, forming cracks which reveal the underlying basecoat colour. Use a flat brush to apply the crackle medium over the basecoat. Leave for twenty minutes to an hour and then, with quick brush strokes or sponging, apply an even coat of contrasting colour. Do not re-apply paint after the crackling starts. Apply a thick coat of paint for large cracks and a thin layer for fine cracks.

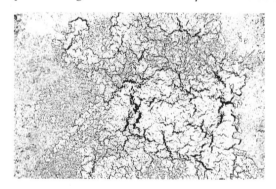

## SPATTERING AND THREAD DRAGGING

This ageing process is applied after the design is dry and before the finish is applied. Add water to paint for a very thin consistency. Dip a toothbrush into the paint and carefully stroke the bristles away from the article, so that spatters of paint hit the desired area. For thread dragging, dip the end of a length of heavy sewing thread in thinned paint and slap the loaded thread against the painting surface.

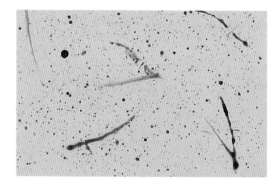

## WOODGRAINING

Woodgrain effect can be achieved using a *kleister* medium or the following paste recipe: mix two tablespoons of cornflour with one tablespoon of cold water to form a smooth paste. Add a cup of boiling water and whisk. Allow to cool, stirring occasionally. Store in a cool place for up to five days. Basecoat the wood a suitable colour: red oxide to imitate mahogany or yellow-based paint for oak or walnut. When basecoat is dry, paint kleister medium or paste thinly over the surface and allow to dry. Mix four parts of paste or medium to one part of brown acrylic, such as burnt umber. Mask off the area to be woodgrained and brush the mixture on a small section. Use a tool—crumpled newspaper, a cardboard comb or a graining rocker—to mark the paste. Soften sharp lines with a sea sponge. Remove tape and clean up edges. For further illustration, see page 41.

## VARNISHING

Before varnishing an article, erase pencil lines and remove dust with a tack cloth. Use a soft flat brush to apply varnish and work in a dust-free environment. Most pieces in this book have been varnished with a satin polyurethane varnish. Apply two coats (or more for added protection) and lightly sand with a medium grade sandpaper between coats, allowing each to dry for twenty-four hours.

For gloss varnishing or imitation lacquer use a high gloss polyurethane varnish and work under adequate lighting. Do not shake varnish, as this creates bubbles. Apply varnish in long even strokes in one direction. Remove air bubbles with gentle overstrokes. Allow to dry for at least twenty-four hours in a dust-free environment. Before applying the next coat, remove the sheen by rubbing in one direction using wet-and-dry paper and detergent. Wipe clean. Apply the second coat of varnish with brushstrokes in the opposite direction. Repeat until you have ten coats.

## ANTIQUING

During the antiquing process, oil paint is applied on areas of an article. Burnt umber is the colour most commonly used, but you might consider using Paynes grey on a blue-grey background or burnt sienna on a red background. A patina is also required to help spread the oil paint evenly over the surface. Commercial antiquing patinas are available or you can make your own by mixing three parts of gum turpentine with one part of linseed oil. As this mixture is highly combustible, it is advisable to wear surgical gloves during the process and to dispose carefully of any cloths used.

Allow the painted article to dry for twenty-four hours before antiquing. Using a soft cloth, lightly wipe patina on to the surface. Add a few drops of the patina to the oil paint and then paint a small amount of this oil paint on to selected areas with a #8 bristle brush. Remove excess paint with a paper tissue. Use a clean soft cloth to rub the remaining oil paint into the cracks and corners. If you are working on wood, rub with the grain. Allow to dry for several days. The article should be touch dry before it is varnished. For illustrations of these steps, see page 70.

## WAXING AND GOLD WAXING

Apply furniture wax after varnishing using 0000 steel wool. Leave to dry for twenty minutes to an hour, then buff to a gentle sheen with a soft cloth.

Gold wax is sometimes used to enhance the finished article. Rub the wax on to selected areas using either your finger tip or a soft cloth. Leave to dry and then buff with a clean cloth for a rich sheen.

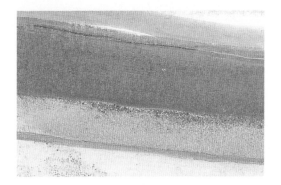

# COLOUR CHART

This chart is a guide for mixing the colours used in the projects. To mix every colour, you will need each of the basic colours shown. Keep in mind, however, that many commercial brands carry a wide range of colours that save you the trouble of mixing your own.

When mixing light colours, start with the lightest basic colour and add portions of darker colours until you have matched the colour swatch. Always test your colour by allowing a small patch to dry first, as acrylic colours tend to dry a shade darker.

It should also be noted that there are some subtle shade variations in some of the projects. Adjust colours by adding a dark toner or white. Where a wash is required, dilute the paint with water.

## BASIC COLOURS

| | | | |
|---|---|---|---|
| *RED* | *CRIMSON* | *PINK* | *YELLOW* |
| *YELLOW OXIDE* | *RAW SIENNA* | *BURNT SIENNA* | *BURNT UMBER* |
| *PURPLE* | *ULTRA BLUE* | *PTHALO BLUE* | *BLACK* |
| **WHITE** | *SILVER* | *GOLD* | *COPPER* |

# PROJECT COLOURS

*XMAS RED*
1 part red
1 part crimson

*FIRE RED*
3 parts red
1 part yellow

*TOMATO*
4 parts red
1 part burnt sienna
1 part yellow oxide

*PIMENTO*
3 parts red
1 part burnt umber

*RED OXIDE*
3 parts crimson
3 parts burnt umber

*DARK BROWN*
4 parts burnt umber
1 part black

*PEACH*
4 parts white
1 part red
1 part yellow oxide
touch of burnt sienna

*ORANGE*
1 part yellow oxide
1 part red

*CINNAMON*
5 parts burnt sienna
2 parts white
2 parts red
1 part yellow

*RUST*
2 parts burnt sienna
1 part red

*BROWN EARTH*
6 parts burnt sienna
1 part burnt umber

*BROWN*
4 parts burnt sienna
1 part burnt umber

*SALMON*
8 parts white
1 part red
touch of yellow oxide

*APRICOT*
8 parts white
1 part yellow oxide
touch of red

*ROSE PINK*
8 parts white
1 part crimson
1 part red

*MAUVE*
4 parts white
1 part ultra blue
1 part crimson

*GRAPE*
4 parts white
2 parts crimson
1 part ultra blue

*CHARCOAL*
2 parts ultra blue
1 part black
1 part burnt umber

*STRAW*
4 parts white
2 parts yellow oxide
2 parts yellow
1 part burnt umber

*SUNFLOWER*
1 part yellow
1 part yellow oxide

*OLIVE*
3 parts yellow
2 parts black
1 part red

*SPRUCE*
3 parts ultra blue
1 part yellow

*TEAL*
3 parts pthalo blue
1 part yellow

*PRUSSIAN BLUE*
4 parts ultra blue
1 part black

*IVORY*
5 parts white
1 part yellow oxide
1 part burnt umber

*PINE*
3 parts white
1 part yellow oxide

*OLD GOLD*
4 parts yellow
1 part black
1 part red

*FOREST GREEN*
3 parts ultra blue
1 part yellow

*AQUA*
3 parts white
1 part pthalo blue
touch of yellow

*FRENCH BLUE*
4 parts white
1 part ultra blue
touch of black

*CREAM*
5 parts white
1 part yellow oxide

*GREY*
4 parts white
1 part black

*OATMEAL*
4 parts white
1 part burnt umber

*MINT*
5 parts white
1 part yellow
1 part ultra blue

*SLATE BLUE*
2 parts white
2 parts ultra blue
1 part burnt umber

*DUSTY BLUE*
5 parts white
1 part ultra blue
touch of black

## AFRICAN POT *(repeat designs)*

## MEXICAN CHAIR

# MOROCCAN SHOEBOX

*lid*

*back*

*front*

*sides*

TURKISH CHEST  (repeat design)

149

*BERRY PICKER (repeat design)*

*GERMAN CHEST*

# SWISS WALL CUPBOARD

*top scroll*

*panel*

*sides*

*bottom scroll*

# AUSTRIAN CHEST OF DRAWERS

*drawers*

*sides*

*chair*

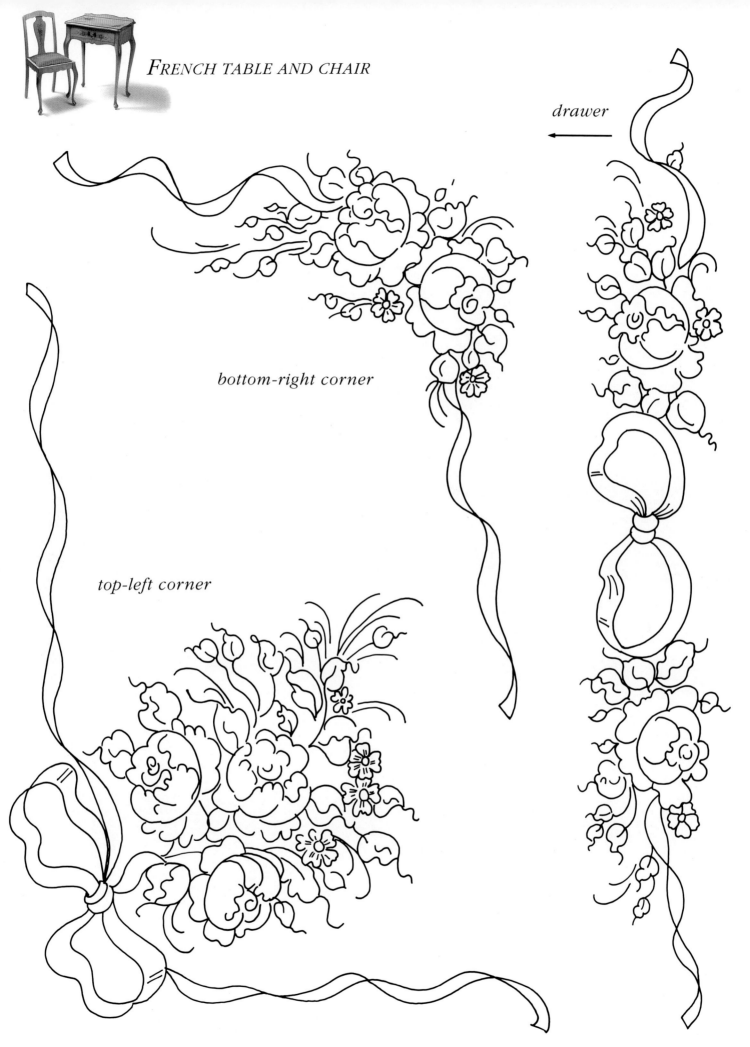

# FRENCH TABLE AND CHAIR

*drawer*

*bottom-right corner*

*top-left corner*

# ROCOCO JEWELLERY BOX

*top*

*front and back*

*ends*

S*WEDISH CHAIR*

*top slat*

*other slats (stagger in size)*

155

*left cupboard door*

*(flop for right cupboard door)*

→

*drawer (symmetrical design)*

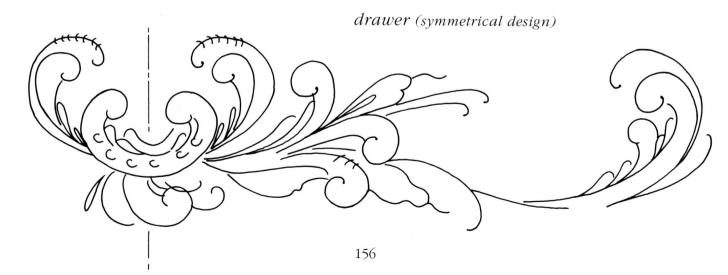

*front panel* (symmetrical design)

*sides*

*legs*

*top*

*side flaps*

159

# HINDELOOPEN BUTTE

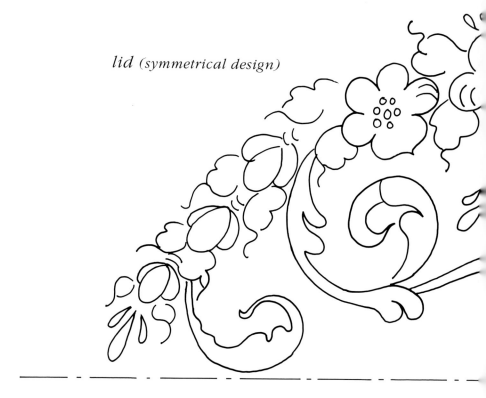

*lid (symmetrical design)*

*sides*

*box front and back*

coffee pot

box ends

164

ITALIAN PLATTER

*centrepiece*

*rim (symmetrical design)*

EASTERN LACQUERWARE

MILK CHURN

*side trim*

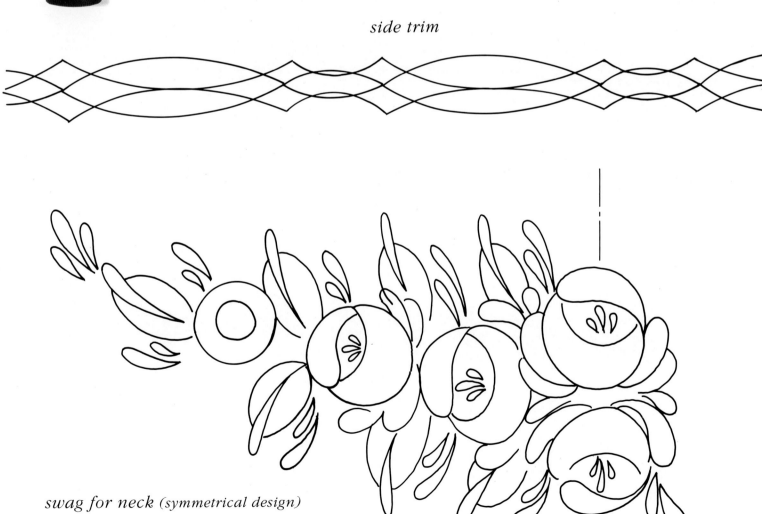

*swag for neck (symmetrical design)*

*garland and panel*

# GLOSSARY

**acanthus**: An ornate leaf shape borrowed from ancient Greek design.

**anthemion**: A stylized honeysuckle borrowed from classical Greece by neoclassical painters.

**antiquing**: The application of paint and a medium to give a piece an aged and mellow appearance.

**arabesque**: An Islamic motif of leaves which twine in and out of a continuous stem.

**armoire**: A wardrobe or cupboard.

**ashphaltum**: A mixture of ashpalt and varnish applied over tin to produce a semi-transparent brown background.

**Baroque**: A style which appeared in Europe in the mid-seventeenth century and was characterized by ornate but symmetrical design.

**Biedermeier**: A style of decoration which flourished in Germanic countries in the early nineteenth century and which favoured imitation woodgrains over painted motifs.

**Bauernmalerei**: A style of folk painting that developed in southern Germany, Switzerland and Austria and is characterized by contrasting colours and naive designs of flowers, birds and people.

**block**: To paint an area of a design in a flat, undiluted colour.

**bride box**: A small round or oval-shaped box which was presented to a bride, particularly among German communities (see spanschachtel).

**brulage au fer**: The decoration of unpainted wood with a hot poker.

*American bride box*

**butte**: The name used in the Netherlands for a food box, usually oval in shape and with a handle on the lid.

**'C' stroke**: A curved brushstroke with a sharp tail at either end.

**cabriole**: A chair (or table) leg that curves in an S-shape and was popular during the Rococo period.

**cartouche**: A circular or shaped panel surrounded by leaves or scrolls and containing a coat of arms, a scene or an inscription.

**chinoiserie**: Pieces decorated in imitation of Chinese art. This fashion, which was particularly strong in France, coincided with the Rococo movement.

*Chinoiserie design*

**codices**: Pictorial manuscripts painted by ancient Mexican artists on deerskin or bark.

**comma stroke**: The basic brushstroke in folk painting, which has a blunt head and a trailing tail.

**crackling**: A painted finish which gives an appearance of age, achieved by applying a crackle medium to a surface.

**Dala horse**: A carved horse traditionally painted red or blue, made in the Dalarna area of Sweden.

**distress**: A finish which suggests age through wear, achieved by sanding selected areas of paint.

**double-loading**: The technique of loading first one colour and then a second colour onto the brush to form blended brushstrokes.

**dower chest**: A large wooden chest which held the handiwork of young women and formed part of the bridal dowry among Pennsylvania Dutch.

**dry brushing**: The application of paint with a dry brush to add character.

**flat brush**: A brush with squared-off bristles.

**fleur-de-lys**: A stylized lily flower or iris motif which became the emblem of the French royalty.

**float**: To paint a wash of colour that fades along one edge of the brushstroke, achieved by side-loading the brush.

**fraktur**: An illustrated certificate painted in watercolours by the Pennsylvania Dutch to mark important occasions.

**gesso**: A thick white undercoat used as a primer on fibreboard and other surfaces.

**glaze**: An application of a semi-transparent colour over bare wood (also called 'staining').

**gourd**: Fruit from the calabash tree which, when dried and hollowed, serves as a container. It is commonly decorated in Africa and Mexico.

*Decorated gourd*

**Gustavian style**: A sophisticated style of decoration favoured by Sweden's Gustavus III, characterized by clean lines and soft colours.

**Hallingdal**: A region in Norway which produced a distinct style of rosemaling.

**hex signs**: Geometric decorations painted on the gable ends of barns in Pennsylvania to ward off evil.

**Hindeloopen**: A painting style which developed in the Netherlands and which is characterized by rich colours and detailed, swirling designs.

**intarsia**: A sophisticated form of marquetry or wood inlay which was widely imitated by furniture painters during the early nineteenth century.

**jagged brush**: A flat brush with bristles cut at intervals.

**japanning**: The European imitation of Japanese lacquerware by using a varnish.

**Khokhloma ware**: Wooden pieces decorated in the characteristic red, black and gold colours of the Khokhloma district in Russia.

**kleister**: The German name for imitation woodgraining, using a tinted paste and a tool for marking a pattern.

**kurbits**: The tree of life motif which features in many, if not most, Swedish folk paintings.

*A Swedish kurbits*

**liner brush**: A fine round brush used for adding detail.

**load**: To apply paint to the brush.

**malyovki**: Ukrainian paintings made on paper and pasted onto the walls of a home.

**marbling**: The application of a painted finish in imitation of marble stone.

**marquetry**: Inlaid work of different coloured woods in furniture, often imitated in paint.

**masking tape**: A strong paper-backed adhesive tape used for masking off areas and for transferring designs.

**matryoshka**: A series of progressively smaller wooden dolls which first appeared in Russia towards the end of the nineteenth century.

**maulstick**: A padded length of wood for steadying the hand and keeping elbows off wet areas.

**Mora**: A town in the Dalarna region of Sweden famous for its floor-standing clocks, often carved in the shape of a woman.

**motif**: A decorative element which can stand alone or be incorporated into a larger design.

*Naïve Mexican carving*

**naïve**: A simple and unaffected style which may appear amusing in its childlike quality.

**papier-mâché**: A combination of paper pulp and glue which can be moulded into shape and which dries hard to make an ideal painting surface.

**patina**: The tarnish of age; the term also refers to the medium used to achieve this effect when antiquing.

**Pennsylvania Dutch**: The style of folk art which developed among the German immigrants to America and which is characterized by bright colours and motifs such as stars, hearts and tulips.

**Petrikivka**: A distinctive style of painting flowers, developed in a town by that name in Ukraine.

**pickling**: The process of whitewashing bare wood using a pale stain. Pickling solutions are commercially available or can be home-made.

**polygons**: Many-sided geometric shapes which feature often in Islamic design.

**primitive**: Painted in a simple and unaffected manner; some American country painting fits this description.

**psyanka**: The Ukrainian craft of painting hollowed eggs, particularly in celebration of Easter.

*Primitive American*

**quatrefoil**: A leaf with four segments, much used in Mediterranean design.

**rayado**: A form of decoration practised in parts of Mexico, in which a design is scratched in lacquer with a thorn or needle to reveal a coloured basecoat.

**retarder**: A commercial medium for slowing the drying process of acrylic paint (also known as extender) to allow more complex brushwork. Retarder can be added to the paint or applied directly onto the brush before loading.

**rocaille**: The French name for the shell motif that was common in Rococo design.

**Rococo**: An elaborate and asymmetrical style of decorative art which developed out of Baroque and peaked late in the eighteenth century. This style was especially popular in France and Italy.

**Rogaland**: A region in Norway which produced a distinctive style of rosemaling.

**rosemaling**: The folk painting of Norway which developed from the Viking scrollwork and the revival of scroll painting in the Baroque period. Literally, the name means 'rose painting'.

*Rosemaling churn*

**Roses and castles**: The style of folk art unique to the painters of narrow boats in the canal system of Great Britain.

**rough brush**: A well-used brush which no longer holds its shape and is useful for painting bushes and trees.

**round brush**: A paint brush with bristles which form a point.

**sable**: A type of fine brush with natural bristles.

**'S' stroke**: A brushstroke with sharp tail at either end and a twist in the middle.

**scaling**: The technique of changing the size of a design while retaining its relative dimensions.

**side-loading**: The technique of adding two contrasting colours onto a flattened brush so that they remain distinct.

**skrinyas**: Ukrainian storage chests which were frequently painted.

**spanschachtel**: European boxes made of thin wood shavings bent around a mould. Spanschachteln (plural) are often painted with the figures of a bride and groom.

**swag**: A draped decoration, generally of flowers, caught at each end.

**tack cloth**: A piece of cheesecloth impregnated with linseed oil and used for removing dust, especially before gloss varnishing.

**Telemark**: A region in Norway which produced a distinctive style of rosemaling.

**tine**: The Scandinavian name for a wooden food box which is oval in shape and has a handle on the lid.

**tôle peinte**: French term for painted tinware and the origin of the name 'tole painting', sometimes used to refer to folk painting in general.

*Tölzer rose*

**Tölzer rose**: A simple rose motif which became popular in the Bauernmalerei tradition.

**transfer paper**: A type of paper coated with either a dark or light colour on one side and used for transferring designs onto the painting surface.

**trefoil**: A leaf with three segments often used in Indian patterns.

**wash**: To apply diluted paint over an area for a translucent effect, either as a background or within a design.

**wet-and-dry**: Silicon carbide paper which is moistened and used for distressing paint.

**wet-on-wet**: A technique in which highlighting and shading colours are applied to a still wet base colour so that colours blend softly.

**whirligig**: A whimsical wind toy, popular in American country style.

**woodgraining**: The creation of patterns in a tinted paste to imitate the grain of expensive timbers, commonly practised in Germany and other European countries.

**zwaq**: The Moroccan art of painting sandalwood furniture.

*Spanschachtel painted to imitate intarsia*

# CONTRIBUTORS

**Glynne McGregor** trained as a commercial artist and now works as a folk artist from her studio in Australia. She is widely known for her understanding of different decorative painting styles and is in demand for commissions, and to exhibit and teach. Her work has also featured in many magazines and on television. Glynne designed and painted all the projects for this book and prepared the painting stages, borders and the inspirational Designs and Variations pages.

**Judy Alsever** has worked as a decorative artist for twenty-one years and has a shop, Heritage House Art, in the United States. Judy has published several books on Scandinavian folk art, specialising in rosemaling, and teaches throughout America and Canada.

**Serge Couturier** has a wide experience in decoration and is regularly contributes to radio on the subject. His business, Motif Serge Couturier, specialises in fantasy finishes and Serge has recently published a book on painting techniques with Viking O'Neil.

**Anne Hill** lived for many years in the Middle East, where she was responsible for the decoration of major hotels. She has worked on a television documentary for the BBC and now runs a business importing Islamic decorative pieces.

**Helen Jeglic** is the author of two books and numerous magazine articles on folk art and has been awarded the Master Decorative Artist certification by the Society of Decorative Painters in America. Helen conducts seminars throughout the United States, Canada and Australia.

**Anthony Lewery** has made the study of British folk art his area of expertise. Among his books are the successful *Narrow Boat Painting* and *Popular Art*, both published by David & Charles.

**Dirk van de Lindt** trained at the National Academy of Fine Arts in Amsterdam. He has worked on the restoration team at the Rijks Museum and as a professional artist and now teaches both restoration work and traditional Hindeloopen from his studio near Sydney, Australia.

**Chlöe Sayer** spent many years of research and fieldwork in Mexico, resulting in television documentaries, lectures and exhibitions at such venues as the British Museum. She has also written numerous books, including *The Arts and Crafts of Mexico* and *Mexican Patterns*.

**Rose Tanasichuk** teaches decorative painting at her Winnipeg shop, Folk Art Etc. She has written several books including *Petrikivka Painting: A Ukrainian Heritage*, published in the United States, and enjoys painting both traditional and contemporary styles.

# INDEX

# ACKNOWLEDGEMENTS

## PHOTO CREDITS

ii Don Klumpp/The Image Bank; 8 Australian Picture Library/ ZEFA/ZENTRALE F; 9 M. Salas/The Image Bank; 12-13 Adam Bruzzone;14 Ignacio Urquiza; 15 D.W. Hamilton/The Image Bank; 24 and 25 Lisl Dennis/The Image Bank; 32 International Photographic Library; 33 Stockshots/Clifford White; 64 Elizabeth Whiting & Associates/David George; 76 International Photographic Library; 77 (chest & cupboard) The Norwegian Folkmuseum; 85 Harald Sund/The Image Bank; 104 Austral-International; 105 (tiled wall) Stockshots; 105 (clock) International Photographic Library; 106 (tile) Don Klumpp/The Image Bank; 110 International Photographic Library; 122 Nevada Wier/The Image Bank; 123 Stockshots/Philip Little; 128 Austral-International; 129 (collected items & table cupboard) & 131 (cabin block) A. J. Lewery; 132-135 Adam Bruzzone; other photography by Andre Martin.

### Individual pieces painted by:

Diana Brandt - chair on 33; writing box on 34; cupboard on 43
E. Tomason Ellingsplassen - chest on 77
Beverley Jones - tine on 78
Pamela Jones - spanschachtel on 33; cabinet on 43
Else Jepperson - plate on 79
Dirk van de Lindt - clogs on 84; pot on 85; tray & scuttle on 86-7
Kerry Melbye - earrings on 106 and on 175
Glynne McGregor - target on 35; bucket base on 42; scene on 65; plate & bread holder on 66-7; spanschachteln on 93 & 95; tankard on 129; jug on 130

### Sincere thanks to those who gave their expertise, loaned pieces and supplied materials:

Leonie Draper for additional research and text
Mary-Anne Danaher for photography styling
Kathy Nordstrom for preparing and finishing project pieces
Chroma Acrylics for paints for projects
Myart for paints and brushes for projects
Australian Pioneer Village at Wilberforce for use of location
Antiques Avignon, Paddington for arch on 55; clock on 65 and chests on 66 & 93
Bliss, Woollahra for jug &glasses on 108; woven cushion on 28
Joan Bowers Antiques, Paddington for bowls on 118; shutters & cushions on 28
Coral Vangnes for rug on 79
Country Furniture Antiques for fruit on 16
The Design Establishment for lacquer box on 124
Jannie Drayer for bowl on 77
Elsa's Folk Art Studio for plate on 79
Folk Art Studio for woodgrain box on 43; cabinet on 35; butte on 85; box on 86; tine on 78; bowl & box on 111; plate on 112; dolls on 113; mug on 130; boxes on 171 and 173
Gallery Nomad, Paddington for beads on 30; lantern on 28
Annette Gero, Antique & Patchwork Quilts for quilts on 92 & 96
Home & Garden on the Mall for napkins, straw apple & orb on 38; glass plates on 108
IKEA for linen on 48
Interentre Australia for Mexican pieces on 15-17, 20 and 172
Dirk van de Lindt for designs featured on 86-7
Linen & Lace for gold folder on 56
Nazar Gallery, Paddington for samovar on 118
Patchwork Primitive for houses on 93 and 172
Vicky's Fabrics, Edgecliff for tassels on 44; seat fabric on 56